Reader's Digest

Wildlife Watch

Gardens & Parks in Winter

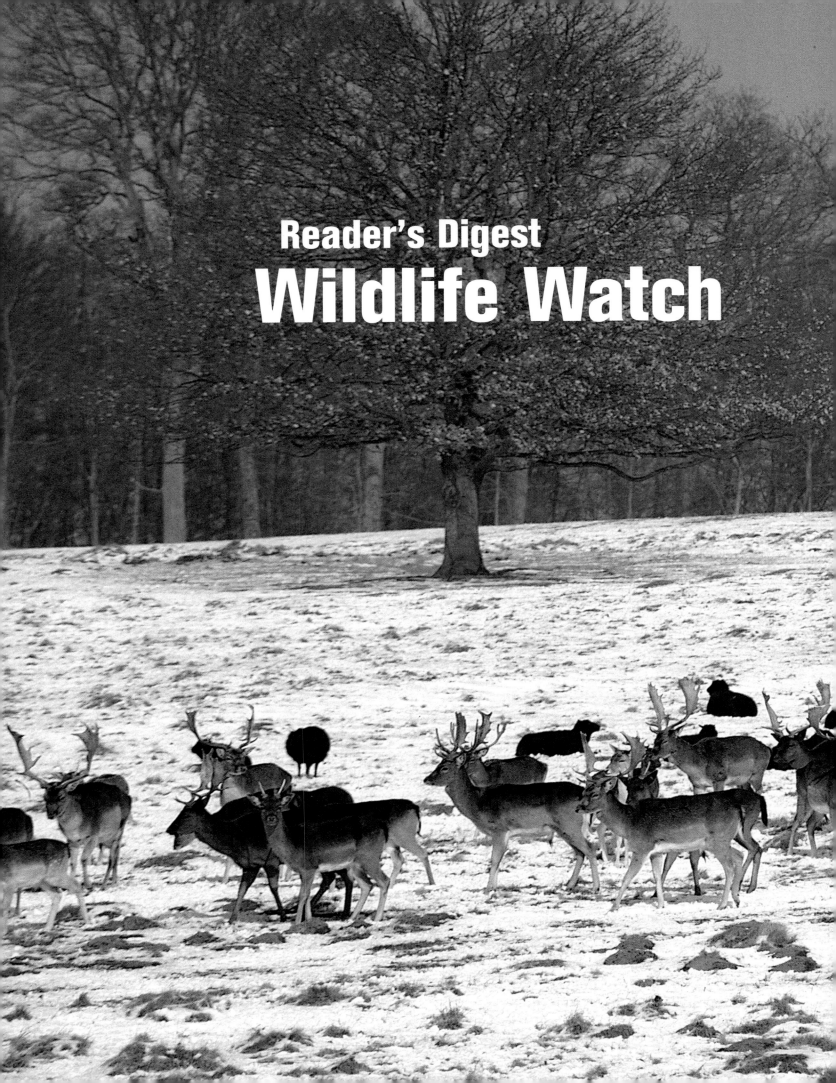

Reader's Digest
Wildlife Watch

Gardens & Parks in Winter

Published by
The Reader's Digest Association Limited
London · New York · Sydney · Montreal

contents

Wildlife habitats and havens

Animals and plants in focus

Garden watch

Park watch

Introduction

A garden on a clear, frosty winter morning can be a magical place. Every leaf has a lacy fringe of ice crystals that glint and sparkle in the low sun, and the grass is blue with frost that squeaks and crunches underfoot. Fence rails appear to steam as they warm up, their veneer of ice turning directly to vapour. Robins sing to defend their winter feeding territories, their feathers fluffed up against the cold, their breath visibly rising from their open beaks.

Gardens and parks are largely deserted – by humans at any rate – and most of the glorious show gardens that are open to visitors in spring and summer simply shut their gates. Yet even though deciduous trees have lost their leaves, herbaceous plants have died down to below ground level and the rich colours of the warmer months seem to have drained away into the cold earth, there is plenty of wildlife to be seen by those prepared to brave the chill.

▲ Mild winter weather can encourage a whole range of plants to flower. The common field-speedwell can often be found blooming in gardens in late December.

◄ Blackbirds, like this female, stay on their garden and parkland territories throughout the year, and often compete with visiting fieldfares and other thrushes for nutritious berry crops.

▼ The bright yellow catkins of hazel appear before the leaves, as early as late January. They are the male flowers of the tree, loaded with pollen that blows away on the wind.

Colourful visitors

Some of the most arresting sights are the newcomers that arrive by air. Many birds that find food scarce in the winter landscape are tempted by the promise of an easy meal at a birdfeeder. Regular garden visitors such as blue tits (see pages 56–61) and great tits are seen in far greater numbers in winter, and species that may rarely visit at any other time, such as woodpeckers, nuthatches and long-tailed tits, often appear in gardens near woodland (see pages 20–23). For many of these birds the energy-rich nuts, seeds and fats put out by garden owners are vital to their survival, and this makes them much more audacious than normal. As a result, they may fall victim to hunting sparrowhawks, which also become increasingly bold as the temperature plummets below freezing.

Meanwhile, berry-bearing shrubs and trees, such as holly (see pages 79–82), are claimed as winter food supplies by mistle thrushes. These big, powerful songbirds can usually chase away smaller competitors, such as blackbirds, but they may be forced to yield to hungry flocks of migrant redwings and fieldfares that often descend on winter gardens along with other thrushes (see pages 99–103). The berries of rowan, pyracantha and other shrubs may also be stripped by occasional invasions of waxwings that have fled the bitter chill and food shortages of the far north.

Storage heater

Other visitors come from closer to home. Gardens and parks in towns are usually some 5°C (41°F) warmer at night than nearby open country, because brick and concrete absorb the sun's warmth during the day and release it at night. Starlings have learned to exploit this urban microclimate, and fly into towns to roost for the night on buildings and parkland trees, often in their thousands. In some cities, pied wagtails take advantage of the same effect, gathering in twittering flocks on the branches of favoured trees. Such mass roosts are an autumn and winter phenomenon, for in early spring the birds disperse to breed. Grassy parks may even attract skylarks in the dead of winter, as well as large numbers of black-headed and common gulls.

▲ The green, bell-shaped flowers of stinking hellebore may appear from early February, providing vital nectar for queen bumblebees that emerge on mild winter days.

▶ Many insects spend the winter as larvae, burrowing deep into the ground. The cockchafer larva feeds on plant roots and grasses, and can cause dead patches on garden lawns.

▶ Ice can make feeding, and even walking, difficult for park waterfowl, such as the mallard, and the birds become more dependent on food provided by human visitors.

The storage-heater effect also benefits many insects that might otherwise perish in the sub-zero temperatures. City gardeners are often surprised to see insects such as queen bumblebees on the wing in December or even January. Some winter-active moths (see pages 71–74) are not only able to survive the cold, but are specially adapted to fly in search of mating partners on the coldest winter nights – an ability that defies the general belief that only warm-blooded animals are able to function in cold conditions. The adult stages of their lives are so short that these moths do not need to feed, so the fact that there are very few nectar-bearing flowers in bloom in winter is no problem for them.

In contrast active bumblebees need nectar to fuel their flight. They are sure to have a fruitless search in many gardens and parks, but if they are lucky they may find winter-flowering native plants such as winter aconite and mezereon (see pages 18–19) as well as a few winter-flowering exotics and cultivars. These plants may get relatively few insect visitors, but any pollen that the insects pick up is very likely to be delivered directly to another plant of the same species, since most other plants are not in flower. This can make winter flowering a surprisingly efficient strategy for plants, provided there are at least some pollinators on the wing. Like the birds and insects, the plants benefit from the winter warmth of urban areas, which protects them from the worst of the frost.

Winter refuges

Although some insects may be active, most adult insects either die or lie dormant in winter. The dormant species may still be encountered, however. Several common garden butterflies hibernate as adults, including brimstones, peacocks and small tortoiseshells. Brimstones nestle in thick growths of ivy, where the male's yellow and the female's greenish white pointed wings blend remarkably well with the ivy leaves. Peacocks and small tortoiseshells favour more sheltered sites, and often find their way into garden sheds where they overwinter in the ideal cool, dry conditions. Old timber sheds can make excellent winter refuges for garden wildlife, especially if they are poorly maintained and rarely visited (see pages 14–17).

In wooded parks many animals may take shelter in the hollow, rotted-out hearts of ancient oaks and other veteran trees (see pages 26–31). Such trees may look almost dead, especially in winter, but they have often survived in this state for hundreds of years. They make ideal retreats for

◀ In winter, the dark, iridescent plumage of the starling is speckled with the white tips of its new feathers. Many parks have vast winter roosts of starlings, with thousands of birds.

▲ The fieldfare often visits gardens and parks in urban areas in hard weather, where it relishes berries and windfall apples.

▲ The tough leaves of brambles are not damaged by frosts, and they can be an important source of winter food for parkland animals, such as deer and rabbits.

overwintering insects and some hibernating mammals, including noctule bats. Other hibernators, such as hedgehogs and hazel dormice, prefer to curl up beneath heaps of fallen leaves, which provide insulation from the freezing temperatures that can threaten their survival (see pages 46–49).

Bright days

Many mammals are active throughout the winter – even tiny, vulnerable-looking creatures such as mice and voles. They can often find plenty of food in the form of seeds and dormant vegetation, and they are small enough to forage beneath the snow in northern regions with regular winter snowfall. This protects them from the winter windchill. It may also conceal them from hungry hunters, including foxes, which are active in many parks and gardens throughout the winter (see pages 40–45). Foxes can often be seen quite easily as they search for prey between the leafless trees of wooded parkland, especially when snow reflects the light back up on to their russet coats.

Much more elusive are the tawny owls that are resident in many town parks (see pages 93–98). They are strictly nocturnal, although an owl can sometimes be located by the angry chatter of small birds 'mobbing' the predator at its daytime roost. Even mammals that normally spend much of the winter asleep, such as squirrels, may emerge to feed on bright, mild days (see pages 84-87). As time wears on, these become more frequent, and the leaf tips of snowdrops – which are specially reinforced for pushing up through frozen soil – start to appear between the fallen leaves of the previous autumn. They are the first flowers of spring, anticipating celandines by a month or more, and although many of the naturalised clumps that grow in parks and gardens may have spread from deliberate plantings, they are often looked upon as native wild flowers. The appearance of their pure white blooms in late January or early February is a sure sign that the deep chill of the season has passed, and that the drab browns and greys that dominate garden and parks in winter will soon give way to the glowing colours of spring.

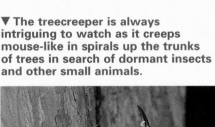

▼ The treecreeper is always intriguing to watch as it creeps mouse-like in spirals up the trunks of trees in search of dormant insects and other small animals.

▲ A native of south-western Ireland, the strawberry tree is widely planted in town parks. Its fruits take a whole year to ripen, and can often be seen in early December.

▲ Although the fallow deer rut is over by late November, the bucks retain their magnificent flat, broad antlers throughout the winter. They lose them in spring, usually one at a time.

Wildlife habitats and havens

- Surviving the cold
- Wildlife in the garden shed
- Winter wild flowers
- Feeding birds in winter
- Life under logs and stones
- Veteran trees
- The Eden Project

Surviving the cold

In the dead of winter, a garden can provide a lifeline for wildlife. Familiar animals are often joined by seasonal visitors that have deserted the leafless woods and frozen fields in their urgent search for food.

Winter is always a testing time for garden wildlife. Low temperatures, which often fall well below freezing, make normal life impossible for amphibians, reptiles and most invertebrates. They also make huge demands on the energy resources of small mammals and birds. To make matters worse, the food that they need to generate energy is often in short supply – even relatively abundant winter food, such as seeds and nuts, becomes scarce as the months progress towards spring.

Some animals deal with the problem by entering a state of hibernation, or passing the winter in a dormant state. Many insect-eating birds migrate to warmer parts of the world where the feeding is better. However, a range of hardy birds, mammals and invertebrates remain active in the winter garden. Emboldened by hunger, they are often easier to watch than at other times of year, and birds, in particular, often come to rely on the food that people put out for them.

Active insects

Some of the most surprising animals to be found in the winter garden are insects. Most insects rely on the warmth of their surroundings to raise their temperature to a level at which their bodies function properly, so in winter they either die or lie dormant. Exceptions to this include various species of bumblebee, which can generate warmth by vibrating their flight

▲ The waxwing is named for the tips of its secondary wing feathers, which resemble pieces of bright red wax. It is nearly always to be seen feeding on red berries.

▶ House flies usually stay indoors in winter but on warm days they may venture into the garden, where they are most likely to be around compost heaps and sheds.

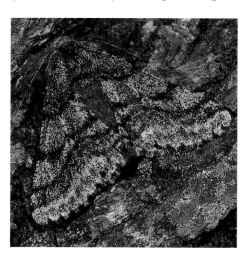

During the day the male brindled beauty moth may be found resting on tree trunks, where its mottled wings provide perfect camouflage against the bark.

muscles without actually taking to the air. On sunny days big queen bumblebees often emerge to sip nectar from winter flowers such as hellebores. Mild spells in winter may also tempt dormant house flies out of their torpor and into the open garden. If mild conditions persist, they may even breed, provided they can find some suitable decaying matter in which to lay their eggs.

Warmer spells are often exploited by a small group of hardy moths. They include the brindled beauty, which may appear as early as February. Since its caterpillars feed on the foliage of lime, apple, willow, hawthorn and silver birch, it is common in gardens, especially in southern and eastern England. Another frequently seen species is the aptly named winter moth. In both these species only the males have wings and look like typical moths. The

females are wingless and, after hatching on the ground, they have to crawl up the trunks of trees to find mates and suitable sites for laying their eggs.

Striking winter visitors

The berry-bearing bushes that provide a splash of colour in the garden in autumn and winter are not just attractive to gardeners. They also attract hungry birds. One of the most exciting is the waxwing. This strikingly crested bird is a winter visitor from Scandinavia and Russia, although the numbers fluctuate considerably from year to year. In most years a hundred or so are seen in Britain and Ireland, but occasionally several thousand may be forced south and west by the failure of berry crops in the north.

◀ Sharp incisor teeth enable the wood mouse to gnaw through the tough shells of nuts scattered beneath garden trees.

▶ Bold face markings, rusty flank and underwing patches distinguish the redwing from the larger song thrush. It is vulnerable to hard winters, and may rely on garden feeding.

Waxwings often turn up in unlikely places, and large flocks may descend on berry-bearing shrubs in suburban gardens. They are remarkably tame and easy to watch as they feed.

The redwing is another winter visitor to Britain, but this species appears far more reliably, arriving between September and November from northern Europe and leaving the following March or April. For much of the time these small yet distinctive thrushes feed in flocks on farmland and grassland, but if heavy frosts or deep snow make their search for earthworms and insect grubs impossible, they may move to gardens where food is more readily available. At such times windfall apples are a welcome addition to their diet.

The most familiar garden bird in winter is almost certainly the robin. Chores such as raking the lawn or digging over a vegetable patch soon attract the curiosity

of this bold, red-breasted resident, and even the most watery winter sunshine may inspire snatches of its sweet, varied song. Unusually, both sexes sing in winter to defend their feeding territories, and perhaps because of this they appear to have little difficulty finding enough natural prey such as insects and worms. However, heavy snowfalls or prolonged periods of freezing temperatures can put this food out of reach, and robins then become more inclined to take food from garden birdfeeders.

Foraging mammals

Despite its name, the wood mouse is common in gardens, even in suburban areas. For much of the year the presence of wood mice is likely to go unnoticed, but during the winter they become more daring, sometimes feeding on fallen nut debris beneath bird tables in broad daylight, or raiding sacks of bird food

stored in sheds. A dusting of snow can often reveal the full extent of their activities, betraying favoured routes through the undergrowth. The tiny footprints occasionally straddle a line in the snow, marking where the mouse's tail brushed the ground.

The most conspicuous mammals to visit winter gardens are usually grey squirrels. These adaptable creatures are quick to exploit any sources of food that a garden may have to offer, becoming increasingly audacious as winter progresses. They often raid birdfeeders and frequently wreck nut or seed containers. Squirrels do not become completely dependent on such handouts, however, since they also forage for fallen nuts and fruits or, more destructively, nibble at swelling buds in late winter. Grey squirrels have even been seen catching a blue tit or great tit that strays too near – a form of opportunism that only adds to their bad reputation.

◀ The inquisitive, yet wary, grey squirrel is renowned for the ingenuity and agility it displays exploiting nuts and other foods left out for garden birds in winter.

WILDLIFE WATCH

How can I help garden wildlife in winter?

● Put out food for the birds, especially high-energy foods such as seeds mixed with fat. Loose seeds also provide vital food for many birds, as well as visiting mice and voles.

● Grow trees and shrubs that bear berries well into winter, such as holly and pyracantha. If you plant them within view of a window, you can watch the birds feeding from the house.

● Leave windfall fruit on the ground, where it will give a sugary boost to birds such as redwings and the occasional winter-flying moth.

● Don't be too tidy in autumn. Many insects such as ladybirds and lacewings use the dead, hollow stems of garden plants as winter refuges, so leaving them in place helps to ensure a healthy insect population the following spring.

Wildlife in the garden shed

For some birds, bees, butterflies and even bats, a garden shed full of flowerpots and old tools can be a perfect haven in which to spend the winter, and maybe even raise a family.

For most gardeners, the shed is a place to store tools and propagate plants. For wildlife, however, it can be an ideal place to live – provided it has the right attributes.

Sheds come in all shapes and sizes, but from the wildlife's point of view the most important feature is the material from which it is made. For insects, birds and mammals, an ideal shed is an old wooden one, preferably rather dilapidated, made of timber that has not been treated with wood preservatives, or at least not for many years. The wood used in most modern sheds is soaked in chemicals formulated to prevent attack by fungi and wood-boring insects. These chemicals are repellent or even lethal to harmless insects such as hibernating butterflies, as well as to the agents of decay. They can also be harmful to larger animals such as bats. Sheds made of brick, concrete slabs or breeze blocks are also less attractive to wildlife than old timber structures. Nevertheless, even the least appealing

shed will offer shelter from the weather, and somewhere to hide from predators during the day, so it may still harbour some interesting creatures.

Rustling butterflies

Old sheds are ideal hibernation sites for overwintering butterflies. The species most commonly found are the small tortoiseshell and the peacock. Both overwinter as adults, sleeping the months away in cool dry places. On warm winter days the hibernating butterflies sometimes betray their presence by a rustling sound as they open and close their wings, but their wings are so well camouflaged when folded that the insects often remain undetected until they start moving about in warmer weather. It is important not to disturb them, since

should they wake up and start flying about, they will waste precious energy, and will not have enough resources to survive the rest of the winter. In spring, butterflies wake of their own accord, and can often be found fluttering against the windows, trying to get out into the garden.

Bats and mice

As the nights get colder, wood mice and yellow-necked mice may take advantage of the shelter offered by a garden shed.

Small tortoiseshell butterflies often hibernate in dry corners of cool garden sheds, their wings folded to conceal their bright patterns and colours.

▼ **All garden sheds, whether neat and well looked after or old and tumbledown, provide shelter from daylight and predators for all sorts of insects, birds, mammals and even amphibians, such as toads.**

◄ The wood mouse is common in gardens throughout Britain, and often uses sheds as winter refuges and breeding sites.

▼ Narrow spaces between wooden boards or beneath the roof are ideal roosting places for tiny pipistrelle bats.

They can be a nuisance, gnawing away at stored bulbs and corms, yet they do no real harm, and do not smell or carry disease. House mice, which are more of a problem and leave a distinctive smell, prefer places with more food.

The yellow-necked mouse is slightly larger than a wood mouse, with a buff-yellow patch on its throat. It is found only in parts of southern Britain, mainly in mature deciduous woods, but it often visits wooded gardens, especially those near large areas of woodland.

Unlike mice, bats hibernate through the winter. Most common are the two species of the pipistrelle, Britain's smallest bats. Small groups or individuals may take refuge in an old shed, squeezing into very small spaces such as the gaps between wooden boards or beneath roofing felt.

They fall into a deeply dormant state, with their body temperature reduced to conserve energy, and metabolic processes slowed to the bare minimum needed to sustain life. This enables them to get through the winter without feeding, although they may emerge to hunt for insects on the wing if the weather is mild enough. As with butterflies, it is essential that they are not disturbed – indeed it is illegal to do so without a special licence.

Web-spinning spiders

Spiders are common inhabitants of dry sheds, especially large, long-legged, fast-moving house spiders. Even a small suburban garden can support up to 20 different species of spider, many of which will seek winter refuge in the shed.

Old cobwebs of web-spinning species soon collect dust and become conspicuous. These can last for months or even years, and often contain what look like spider skeletons – the long legs are dry and stiff and there appears to be no body. These are actually moulted spider skins, discarded as the animals grow. Spiders are completely harmless and many are nocturnal, so they may not be seen by day in the shed unless they are disturbed by

LONG-LEGGED HARVESTMEN

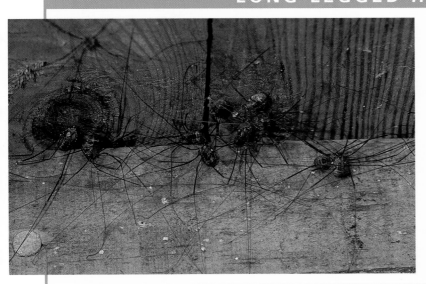

Several types of harvestman can be found in garden sheds. These leggy creatures are often confused with spiders, but they have a different body structure, with the various parts fused into a single pea-like unit. They have eight very long, wiry legs, but since they lose their legs easily if attacked by predators, harvestmen are commonly found with seven, six or even fewer legs. They hunt other small animals, such as insects, spiders and woodlice, so the wildlife in the average garden shed provides them with plenty of prey.

Some species seem to be particularly associated with human activity and turn up regularly in garden sheds. They include *Odiellus spinosus*, which is the bulkiest British harvestman with a body length of up to about 11mm (nearly ½in). Another common shed inhabitant is *Opilio parietinus*, often found resting on the lower parts of brick walls and easily identified by its spotted underside. It frequently occurs with another common species, *Phalangium opilio*, which has short, black-tipped spines dotted over its upper surface.

Sheltered, dampish spots are favoured by harvestmen, and sheds and outbuildings provide them with a perfect environment. They are protected from the elements, with a supply of prey in the form of other insects and invertebrates.

▲ Dilapidated sheds often have gaps that make ideal sites for the orb webs of garden spiders.

► Many sheds are inhabited by large house spiders, which spend most of their time lurking in their dusty sheet webs.

to be human. They are often those of chickens, probably raided from dustbins. Foxes may also store food in the garden, often burying it in flowerbeds with the intention of returning to eat it later.

Destructive woodworm

Woodworm is the scourge of stored timber, especially softwoods, and many old wooden sheds are infested with it. It is actually not a worm at all, but the larva of the furniture beetle. It feeds on dead timber, and is an important decomposer of fallen tree trunks and branches in forests. If it gets the chance, however, it will gnaw a maze of tunnels through the timbers of a shed, severely weakening the structure.

Woodworm tends to get started in damp, dark places, rather than in timbers exposed to the light. This is partly because damp wood attracts fungi which make it softer and easier to eat. The activities of the larvae often go unsuspected throughout the winter until they turn into adult beetles and emerge from the timber, leaving their characteristic tiny holes at the surface. The adult beetles are about the size of uncooked rice grains, and they come out between May and July.

Wasps and bees

Knot holes in shed walls may allow wasps to get in. The shed provides them with space to build their communal nest, as well as the wood that they use to

The damper parts of a shed's timbers may provide food for the wood-boring larvae of the furniture beetle – more commonly known as woodworm.

make it. Wasps rasp away wood with their jaws, then mix it with saliva to make paper pulp, which they use to build the nest walls. By late summer the nest may be bigger than a football, and contain thousands of wasps. Such a nest can be a real problem to a gardener because the worker wasps are likely to attack anyone who goes near it. By winter, however, all the workers have died off, so the nest is empty. Only young mated queens survive, and they may find the shed an ideal place in which to pass the winter undisturbed before starting a new colony in spring.

Various species of solitary bees are able to exploit the smallest cavities in shed walls. The bees make small individual

moving tools or boxes. They are also most likely to be seen in summer, as few are active in winter.

Beneath the floor

Some sheds are raised off the ground, leaving a dry, sheltered space beneath. In winter this makes a perfect refuge for a hibernating hedgehog. It is also ideal for breeding later in the year. The female collects grass, paper and leaves to build a nest, where she will give birth to her young, usually in the spring. The family may remain there for up to six weeks before dispersing.

A sheltered space under a shed is also a favourite site for garden foxes to excavate a den, or earth. Often they too will have their young under the shed, usually in late March. Foxes frequently drag food back to their den, and an accumulation of old bones can build up underneath the shed. These can be a disconcerting discovery if the shed is moved at a later date, but close inspection soon reveals that the bones are too small

One survey found that 40 per cent of foxes living in town gardens used the spaces beneath garden sheds as breeding dens. These also make perfect winter retreats.

◄ A wasps' nest is not the most welcome sight in a garden shed. By winter, however, it will have been abandoned, allowing its wonderful paper structure to be appreciated as a marvel of animal architecture.

► Woodlice are most active by night, in warm weather; they seek dark places to hide during the day and in winter. They have poor eyesight, and are thought to locate food and each other by smell.

▼ Robins are probably the most common birds found in garden sheds. They often select awkward places to nest, and their breeding efforts may then come to grief.

nests, unlike the large communal nests of common wasps or honey bees. The female provisions her nest with nectar and pollen, to feed the larvae that hatch from the few eggs that she lays before she dies. The larvae may stay in the nest for nearly a year before maturing into adults.

Nesting sites
Sheds with broken windows or doors allow birds, such as swallows, to gain access and build their nests. Swallows prefer larger, older, traditionally designed buildings, but they will often make their nests on or near the rafters of sheds, garages and other outbuildings, as well as farm barns. The nest is made largely of mud, so swallows are unlikely to use sheds that are far from water.

Robins may get in, too, especially if a shed door or window is habitually left open. They nest lower down, often in a coil of rope, on a pile of old clothes or dusters, or among stored boxes and tins. It is important not to block their entry route, so if the birds have got in through an open door, put a brick in the doorway to ensure that the door does not blow shut. Remember to remove

Toads cannot survive the winter in the open. They usually hibernate in sheltered underground hideaways, but they may sometimes spend the winter in crevices beneath, or even inside garden sheds.

anything valuable, however, as well as any tools that could be used to break into a house or other building.

Knot holes in cladding planks often provide access to a space between the inner and outer walls of a shed. Blue tits and great tits may nest here if the entrance holes are big enough – 25–29mm (1–1⅛in) across. In winter the birds may use such holes for roosting, since they provide excellent insulation against the winter cold.

Woodlouse refuge
Damp areas of a shed, such as around the wall bases, will attract woodlice. These creatures tend to cluster together, especially in cold winter weather when they are less active. As they are crustaceans, they lack the waterproof skin possessed by insects, so they dry out easily. This is why they prefer damp places. Also, they feed on rotten wood and debris, which is likely to be found at the base of the shed walls. Woodlice are interesting, harmless creatures, and they make useful prey for any toads that may be lurking in dark, damp corners of the shed.

WILDLIFE WATCH

How can I share my shed with garden wildlife?

● Avoid using wood preservers and other chemicals that are poisonous to animal life. You may have to decide which you value most – the shed or the wildlife that lives in it.

● If you find animals hibernating in the shed in winter, be very careful not to wake them up as this will cause them to use up vital stored energy, and they may starve before spring arrives.

● If you need to tidy up the shed, clear it out or repair it, do the job in summer when animals are active outdoors and able to keep out of your way.

● A rarely visited shed may be used by nesting birds in spring. If you need something from the shed, watch for the adults to leave before retrieving it – and don't disturb the nest.

● If your old shed is falling down, and you have the room, consider leaving it to the wildlife and putting up a new one in another part of the garden.

Winter wild flowers

Only a few wild flowers bloom in late winter but several colourful native species can be planted in the garden to brighten a bleak day. They provide vital nectar for early garden insects, such as bumblebees.

Stinking hellebore

Now a rarity in the wild, the stinking hellebore inhabits shallow calcareous (chalk or limestone) soils in a few locations in southern England and Wales. It makes an excellent garden plant, bearing stiff, blue-green, palmate (five-lobed) leaves all year round, and producing clusters of pendulous, bright yellow-green, purple-edged flowers from late January to May, even in the most severe winters. It often seeds prolifically, but the seedlings are easy to weed out and even transplant if required.

The common name of this plant is slightly misleading because it does not have a very unpleasant odour but a stale smell like that left by house mice. It is able to grow in a variety of garden situations, but a moisture-retentive, well-drained soil in partial shade will provide it with the best conditions.

Snowdrop

Well named, since it often blooms while winter snow is still on the ground, the snowdrop is probably the best-known winter flower. The appearance of its delicate, drooping, white heads never fails to raise the spirits, for these flowers anticipate the onset of spring. It is uncertain whether the snowdrop is a native species – it has been cultivated in Britain since the 16th century, but some clumps in the damp woods of the Welsh borders, Somerset and other parts of southern and western Britain may be natural.

Snowdrops are best planted 'in the green', which means as bulbs that are still in active growth after flowering. These may be more expensive than dry bulbs but they tend to survive better. They look best planted in natural-looking clumps.

The lime-green flowers of stinking hellebore are held in sprays above stiff evergreen leaves. The plant may be seen in its full glory on the southern chalk hills, growing among open woodland and scrub rather than grassy downland.

The snowdrop is looked on as a wild flower, yet most of its colonies originated as garden escapes. In the wild, clumps of snowdrops are found growing in damp woodland and beside streams throughout the British Isles, such as here in north Exmoor where they are probably native.

Mezereon or daphne

The rosy-pink, scented flowers of mezereon, borne on leafless stalks as early as February, bring colour to the bleakest days of winter. Also known as daphne, mezereon has become a victim of its own popularity, for although it is a native species, this plant is now a national rarity in the wild. This is mainly because, in the past, it was excessively collected for garden cultivation. Most of these illegally collected plants probably died anyway, as mezereon does not respond well to transplanting.

Wild mezereon grows in woodland and scrub in a few localities from Sussex to Yorkshire. In the garden, the plant prefers a well-drained, humus-rich soil, but tolerates partial shade. Container-grown plants are widely available, but they can also be raised from seed. Mezereon is relatively easy to look after – keep it watered for the first year after planting and prune only to remove dead wood.

◀ Once known as 'paradise plant' because of the heady fragrance of its flowers, mezereon is now rare in the wild, where it is restricted to woodland and scrub on chalk or limestone soils.

▶ Spurge laurel is one of the most handsome plants of chalky woodlands in winter, owing to its drifts of dark evergreen leaves. It also produces clusters of greenish-yellow flowers as early as January.

Spurge laurel

This often underestimated plant blooms with heavily scented, lime-green flowers that appear among the topmost foliage from January to April. Unlike mezereon, a close relative, spurge laurel has shiny evergreen leaves, which make the plant attractive at other times of year as well.

In the wild, spurge laurel grows in woodland on calcareous soils, mainly in southern England where it is more common than mezereon. It is less plentiful in Wales and absent from most of Scotland and Ireland. In the garden, it is an ideal plant to place alongside a well-used path, where the fragrance of its musk-scented flowers can be appreciated. Soil and site requirements are similar to those of mezereon, and provided those conditions are fulfilled, the plants are easy to look after.

In parts of Suffolk the yellow flowers of winter aconite are known as 'choirboys' because of the ruffed appearance of the green bracts below the petals. They open very early in the year, but only if the temperature rises above 10°C (50°F) during a spell of mild winter weather.

Winter aconite

One of the first plants to bloom in the garden is winter aconite, a member of the buttercup family. The bright yellow, cup-shaped flowers, surrounded by ruffles of modified green leaves called bracts, are produced from mid-January. Although not native – it was introduced from southern Europe – naturalised winter aconite can be found growing in woodland all around Britain.

Winter aconite is ideally suited to garden borders and is tolerant of shady places. Plants can be propagated by dividing the tiny, knobbly, underground fleshy roots, called tubers, after flowering. Alternatively, seeds can be collected in spring and sown the following autumn, although it will be a few years before the plants are large enough to flower.

WILDLIFE WATCH

How can I grow winter-flowering native plants?

● Good garden centres should stock many of these plants. Many species are also advertised in the national gardening press in early spring, and can be purchased by mail order.

● Try Chiltern Seeds, Bortree Stile, Ulverston, Cumbria LA12 7PB. Telephone 01229 581137 or visit www.edirectory.co.uk/chilternseeds.

● The Royal Horticultural Society's *RHS Plant Finder* is updated annually and provides information on where to buy more than 73,000 plants, including many native species. It is available from bookshops or the RHS at 80 Vincent Square, London SW1P 2PE. Telephone 020 7834 4333 or visit www.rhs.org.uk/rhsplantfinder/plantfinder.asp

Feeding birds in winter

Wild birds often struggle to survive cold temperatures. Putting out food and water can make all the difference, attracting greenfinches, tits, starlings, blackbirds and even the occasional woodpecker.

Many different small songbirds visit the garden when food is available. In winter the species mix with just the occasional squabble over tasty titbits.

Great spotted woodpeckers will visit all manner of feeders to find peanuts. Wedging the nuts into crevices in tree bark or posts will attract them, along with nuthatches – but make sure the nuts are jammed in tightly to stop them being pulled out and swallowed whole or taken away to hoard.

Many people feed wild birds as a way of attracting them to the garden and watching them at close quarters, but garden feeding actually plays a vital part in the birds' survival, especially in winter.

The value of winter feeding has been known for a long time. It can literally make the difference between life and death for many birds. However, feeding them all year round gives birds a better chance of surviving periods of food shortage whenever these may occur, whether in winter, during summer droughts, or during the spring breeding season. Breeding females in particular need plenty of nutrients for making eggs and to provide the energy they need to gather food for their hungry broods of young.

It is important to remember that birds quickly start to rely upon garden feeding as a vital source of food. So once the birds start coming, try to keep up the supply by putting out food and water regularly – twice daily if possible. This will attract more individual birds and encourage a greater variety of species. By choosing the menu carefully, and offering it in a

variety of ways, it is possible to meet the needs of a wide range of species and reduce competition between them. It also increases the chances of attracting birds that rarely visit typical birdfeeders.

Cleanliness is important, too. Never allow uneaten food to accumulate around the feeders, and clean the feeders themselves whenever they are dirty. Move the feeders regularly, since this reduces the risk of ground-feeding birds picking up parasites and diseases from spilled food that has been contaminated with droppings from birds feeding above.

Popular peanuts

Of all the foods put out for birds, peanuts are without doubt the most widely available – and among the most popular with a variety of birds. They are best offered in a wire-frame feeder rather than loosely scattered, mainly because this prevents their wholesale removal by squirrels and larger birds, such as jackdaws and magpies. Also, it is easier for birds to peck at nuts held in place by the weight of the nuts above, and it eliminates the risk of smaller birds attempting to swallow them whole and choking on them. Avoid using the plastic mesh bags

◄ Perching on the edge of a birdbath, a starling takes a careful look around before beginning to bathe. Birds busy bathing or with wet feathers can be at serious risk from predators, especially domestic cats.

► A nuthatch gets its bill into a home-made fat ball, rich in nutritious seeds. Such mixtures are excellent for winter feeding because they provide plenty of the energy that birds need to keep out the cold.

that the peanuts may be sold in – birds can trap their feet in the mesh, and a squirrel can chew the bottom out of the bag and empty it in a matter of seconds.

Peanuts are rich in oil and protein. The oil provides an almost instant source of energy, while the protein is useful for growing and moulting. Opinions used to differ about the suitability of supplying birds with peanuts throughout the year. Some recommended that peanuts should not be put out after March on the grounds that whole peanuts are dangerous for young nestlings. However, most authorities, including the RSPB and the British Trust for Ornithology, now encourage year-round feeding, provided that the nuts are retained in a feeder that prevents the removal of whole nuts.

Seeds and cereals

Throughout the winter months, a wide variety of birds forage for weed seeds and grain in the countryside at large. Modern farming practices do not encourage weeds or spilt grain, however, and many stubble fields are now ploughed and reseeded with winter crops by autumn. As a result, many farmland birds have come to rely on the cereal grains and mixed seeds provided in garden feeders during the winter. Finches, buntings and tits, as well as sparrows, can be encouraged by placing the seeds in a feeder equipped with perches. Special feeders are available for the small black niger seed favoured by fine-billed goldfinches, and since in winter these exquisite birds feed in small flocks – aptly named 'charms' – they are well worth luring into the garden.

Feeders with perches are preferable because seeds placed on a bird table will be found by larger birds, such as pigeons, which may deter smaller birds. Pigeons need not go without, though, for they can gather any seeds that are spilled on the ground. In rural areas these may also attract pheasants. Such ground-feeding birds are helpful, since they remove the seeds before they can sprout.

OPPORTUNIST SQUIRRELS

Grey squirrels are not usually welcome at garden feeders or bird tables because of the vandalism they inflict. A squirrel is quite capable of gnawing through plastic or even wire, and will make short work of anything made of wood. Squirrels also have big appetites, and will soon clear a bird table of seeds and nuts. Scattering food in the open or fitting a conical-shaped squirrel deterrent to the post supporting the bird table, may help prevent raids. Known as baffles, these deterrents may be bought from bird food suppliers.

A grey squirrel helps itself to a meal. Once it learns that food is available, it will keep coming back for more.

HOW TO FEED BIRDS

● **BIRD TABLES** A bird table needs a raised rim to retain the food, with a gap at the corner for clearing away uneaten scraps. Drill a few holes in the tray for water drainage. A basic roof will keep off the heaviest rain but may deter more wary species.

● **NUT FEEDERS** Soft plastic nets are best avoided, but metal mesh feeders are safe to use, as are feeders made of sheet metal with holes. The mesh or holes should measure about 6mm (¼in) – large enough to stop birds damaging their beaks, yet small enough to prevent them removing whole nuts.

● **SEED FEEDERS** Those with perches are suitable for feeding sunflower mixes; special versions are available for the small niger seed favoured by goldfinches. Feeders that have trays or flat surfaces are fine for cereal-based mixes but they must be cleaned out regularly.

● **HOME-MADE DEVICES** Coconut halves and tit bells filled with fat or bird cake can be hung upside down from a bird table, the branches of a tree or a wall bracket to attract greenfinches, house sparrows and tits.

● **OTHER IDEAS** Fill the holes and cracks of a post or a suspended log with food for agile and insect-eating birds. In wooded areas, try using fat, which may attract woodpeckers and nuthatches. Scatter food on the lawn for ground-feeders, spacing it out to reduce competition between the feeding birds. If there is snow on the ground, clear small areas before putting down the food.

Coconut halves are ideal for agile blue tits. When empty, the shells can be re-filled with fat or bird cake.

SUITABLE FOODS

Special bird foods

● **Birdseed mixture** Avoid seed mixtures containing split peas, beans, dried rice, lentils or dog biscuit (pink or green lumps), because they need to be soaked before birds can eat them. Mixes that contain whole peanuts should be offered only in small-mesh feeders.

● **Black sunflower and niger seeds** In many areas, some birds seem to prefer these to peanuts.

● **Peanuts** Never use salted peanuts, and always buy from a reputable dealer who will guarantee that the nuts are free from aflatoxin, a natural substance carried by a mould fungus, which can kill birds.

● **Coconut** Fresh, not desiccated, this is very popular with tits. Simply rinse out any remaining sweet coconut water and hang up the half shell.

● **Mealworms and waxworms** These are relished by robins and other insect-eating birds and are commercially available.

Store-cupboard favourites

● **Bread** Crumbled, and moistened if very dry.

● **Pastry** This can be fed to birds either cooked or 'raw'.

● **Rice** Cooked, with no salt; brown rice is more nutritious than white.

● **Oats** Either dry porridge oats or coarse oatmeal.

● **Fat** All types of animal fat are suitable, except salty bacon rind; avoid polyunsaturated vegetable fat.

● **Bird cake** Make bird cake by pouring one cup of melted suet or lard onto two cups of mixed seeds, nuts, dried fruit, oatmeal, cheese and cake.

● **Cheese** Try mild, hard cheese, preferably grated.

● **Bones** These should be suspended well out of reach of cats and dogs.

● **Potatoes** Cooked any way except chipped (unless the chips have been fried in lard or dripping and not salted).

● **Fruits** Fresh or dried – even partly rotten fruit is eaten.

Fat balls

Fat – preferably lard or dripping – is one of the most important sources of winter food for birds in the garden. Not only is it a high-energy food in its own right, but it also provides a medium into which seeds, nuts and other food materials can be embedded. Such 'fat balls' can be home-made using a mixture of melted hard fat and seeds, or bought ready-made. Hang them well out of reach of animals on the ground to deter any local cats, dogs, foxes and rats.

Another way of using fat is to smear it onto a post or – ideally – into holes and crevices in an old tree stump. With luck this will attract great spotted woodpeckers, long-tailed tits, nuthatches, goldcrests, wrens and treecreepers. Put the fat on the north-facing side of the timber to prevent the sun melting it.

Windfall fruit

Fruit is one of the favourite foods of many birds, as well as garden mammals and insects. In the wild, fruit is mostly available in late summer and autumn, and it is worth saving some windfall apples for later in the year. Stored in a cool, dry place the apples will keep for months, and when frost and snow cover the ground in midwinter, the fruit will be much appreciated by garden birds.

Thrushes – song and mistle thrushes, blackbirds, redwings and fieldfares – are particularly partial to apples, but robins

A well-stocked garden bird table provides a lifeline for birds during the winter months, when other food is hard to find.

Water for drinking and bathing is as important to birds as food, even in winter, because they have to keep their plumage clean and healthy throughout the year.

and tits are attracted too if the weather is bad. A few insects, such as beetles and winter-flying moths, visit fruits. Grey squirrels, wood mice and brown rats will also soon find them. To discourage rats, take the apples in at night.

Birds and water

Wild birds need year-round access to water – even garden birds that are not usually associated with watery habitats. They need to drink regularly and they need water to keep their plumage clean. Water helps to loosen dirt from their feathers, and may remove parasites as well. After bathing, a bird will preen, reapplying oil to its plumage from the preen-gland at the base of the tail.

Birds will use almost any source of clean water and a simple bath can be made from an old dish or an upturned dustbin lid. Place a few stones in the base to provide perches. Keep it clean and change the water regularly – daily in warm weather.

The bath should be carefully positioned because birds are vulnerable to attack by cats when bathing or drinking. A bird-bath raised above the ground on its own pedestal is often safest, but if the bath is at ground level, make sure that it is sited well away from ground-covering vegetation – otherwise the birds may be ambushed as they bathe.

Preventing freezing

If the temperature drops below freezing, remember to break the ice regularly and remove the fragments. Adding hot, but not boiling, water at frequent intervals can help, and lining the bath with polythene enables ice to be removed easily. Never add anti-freeze, salt or other chemicals to the water to stop it freezing, because this will damage the birds' plumage, and may even poison them.

Ice can be prevented from forming by heating the water indirectly, using a waterproof cable connected to a light bulb underneath the bath. This uses a lot of energy, though, and is effective only if the bath is made from metal. A thermostatically controlled aquarium heater wedged into a pile of pebbles in the bottom of the bath is more efficient.

A garden pond can be made bird-friendly by ensuring that it has a shallow end, with a gradual increase in depth, or better still a very shallow bay, almost cut off from the main pond. Perches close to the surface can be provided by strategically placed boulders, or branches or logs.

What birds will visit?

The most likely visitors to bird tables in winter are blue tits, great tits, blackbirds, robins, greenfinches, starlings, house sparrows and collared doves. Dunnocks, song thrushes and chaffinches will hop around on the ground below. In more wooded areas, a birdfeeder may attract great spotted woodpeckers, nuthatches and coal, marsh, willow and long-tailed tits. Blackcaps are also becoming frequent visitors to some winter bird tables. Mistle thrushes, fieldfares and redwings visit gardens for fruit and berries. In south-east England, bird tables may even attract feral ring-necked parakeets – a spectacular reward for feeding the birds in winter.

Peanuts are best served in metal feeders as the nuts cannot be extracted whole from them and they also deter squirrels. Plastic mesh bags can be dangerous, trapping the feet of small birds.

The robin is one of the most regular garden visitors. It eats mainly animal matter, and has a taste for suet and cheese, but its favourite food is mealworms.

WILDLIFE WATCH

How can I help garden birds?

● The Royal Society for the Protection of Birds (RSPB) can offer information and advice, and publishes a booklet *The Birds in Your Garden*. Contact the Society on 01767 680551 or visit www.rspb.org.uk

● The RSPB also organises the annual nationwide 'Big Garden Birdwatch', in which observers record the number of each bird species seen over one hour. The results enable researchers to judge nationwide trends in bird populations. For details telephone the RSPB on the above number, or visit www.rspb.org.uk/birdwatch/index.asp

● The British Trust for Ornithology (BTO) runs a Garden BirdWatch survey based on weekly reports by participants, submitted on paper or online. For details, telephone 01842 750050 or visit www.bto.org/gbw/

Life under logs and stones

Cavities beneath logs and stones make ideal retreats for insects, slugs and snails that need to hide from the light or hungry predators. Simply turning over a stone can reveal a whole secret society of wildlife.

Animals that inhabit the perpetually dark environment beneath logs and stones – or under bricks, planks of wood and sheets of corrugated iron – fall into two main categories. There are those that normally burrow through the soil, for which the earth under a stone is just an extension of their usual habitat. This includes earthworms and a number of burrowing centipedes and millipedes, as well as small insects that feed underground and use earthworm burrows as convenient corridors through the soil.

Then there are animals that spend the daylight hours hidden beneath logs and stones, but come out at night to hunt or feed. This group includes a number of spiders, woodlice, centipedes, millipedes, slugs, snails and ground-dwelling insects, such as many common beetles.

All these creatures take advantage of the shelter offered by logs and stones for a variety of reasons. The most obvious of these is that the tough, physical barrier protects them from the searching eyes or noses of predators, such as thrushes, blackbirds, robins, shrews and hedgehogs, all of which eat a wide range of invertebrate prey.

Dark, damp hiding places are also good for creatures that are sensitive to the sun's damaging rays. Earthworms,

for example, are often found under stones because their moist skins dry out very easily, and they are sensitive to the ultraviolet light radiated by the sun. This radiation – which also causes sunburn and skin cancer in humans – may be fatal to exposed earthworms.

▲ Several types of millipede live under stones and logs. This particular species, *Tachypodilius niger*, has the distinctive habit of curling up when disturbed.

▲ Here, lifting a stone has revealed a number of woodlice and round snails. Both types of animal prefer to stay in moist, sheltered places by day, and since they are so small the microhabitat beneath a cool stone makes an ideal refuge.

▲ Hairy snails are quite common in gardens, living beneath stones and emerging at night or in damp weather to feed. Unfortunately the 'hairs', which are very fine extensions of the shell, often get rubbed off, making the creatures more difficult to identify.

▲ Unlike their relatives the snails, slugs do not have large shells into which they can retreat from the sun or predators. Species like this leopard slug live beneath stones, such as paving slabs, and emerge at night or on dull days to feed – in this case on some fungus growing on dead wood.

◀ These tiny white woodlice live only in the nests of yellow meadow ants, feasting on the edible debris that accumulates in the nest passages and chambers.

▶ Smooth newts often hibernate beneath logs and stones. During the summer they also spend the daylight hours hidden away from the drying rays of the sun, which could be fatal.

Slugs, snails and newts appreciate the damp conditions, too. Newts are often thought of as pond dwellers, but outside the breeding season they spend their lives away from water, living beneath stones and emerging at night to hunt for small animals. Like frogs and toads, they are amphibians and risk losing vital body moisture through their thin, permeable skins if they come out by day.

Warm spots

Although logs and stones in shady places create cool, damp conditions, exposed stones in sunny spots warm up and retain heat during the night, so they can provide refuges for animals that like to be warmer. These include the woodlouse spider, recognisable by its reddish orange legs, pale abdomen and long armour-piercing fangs. It prefers a warm and only slightly damp place to live and search for its woodlouse prey, so the ground beneath a sun-warmed stone is ideal.

Such refuges may stay warmer than the surrounding ground during the colder months, and are often sought at this time by animals that do not normally live under stones, but retreat beneath them to escape the rigours of winter. This winter protection is exploited by colonies of black and red garden ants, which often make their nests under suitable stones. The shelter enables ants to survive winter frosts, and emerge at the first sign of spring. Yellow meadow ants occasionally nest beneath stones, and their nests frequently contain blind white woodlice, which scavenge for food in the nest galleries. They are tolerated by the ants because they help to keep the nest clean by removing detritis that might otherwise be a source of infection and disease.

Temporary refuges

Some larger animals may also be found beneath stones or logs. During the summer it is not unusual to find a common toad taking shelter there,

or – in drier conditions – a slow-worm. Toads may hibernate beneath large stones in winter for security and insulation against frost.

Even small mammals take advantage of suitable spaces beneath stones. Moving a large stone or log occasionally reveals the nest of a field vole. If it is full of babies, it is essential not to touch them, in case the mother deserts the nest.

▲ Colonies of black garden ants spend the long winter months beneath stones and paving slabs. The adult workers and larvae huddle together, waiting for the warmth of the spring sun to penetrate their refuge.

◀ Common toads are often found underneath stones during the day, waiting for nightfall when they emerge to hunt among cool, moist vegetation. These cavities may also serve as secure hibernation sites in winter.

WILDLIFE WATCH

What will I find under logs and stones?

● Any stone, log, brick, tile, concrete slab or metal sheet already lying in the park or garden is likely to conceal small animals. Try placing extra shelters in a variety of shaded and sunny spots to encourage more wildlife to take up residence.

● A pile of logs, often found in parks, may be used as a hibernation site by toads and insects. Try keeping a log heap in the garden.

● A sheet of old vinyl flooring, carpet or other insulating material covering a compost heap creates ideal warm, moist conditions for the small animals that help to decompose the compost, as well as larger creatures such as slow-worms.

● Whenever looking under logs, stones or any other shelter, remember to replace them, taking care not to crush the animals beneath. They must not be exposed for too long or they may dry out and die.

Veteran trees

Many old parks and woods contain trees that have survived for hundreds of years. Gnarled, contorted and sometimes hollowed out by age and rot, these battered giants are living nurseries for new generations of wildlife.

When winter strips trees of their leaves, the form of each tree is revealed with stark clarity. In any ancient parkland or wood, it soon becomes apparent that certain trees are quite unlike those that surround them. They are often misshapen, with strangely knotted and contorted limbs, great bosses on their trunks, and ragged snags of dead timber. Their most distinctive features, however, come from their massive proportions. Overall they may not be very large, having lost many of their branches, but their trunks are often gnarled pillars of immense girth, often hollow but still capable of bearing new leaves each spring. The sheer breadth of such a trunk is an indicator of great age, of four centuries or more.

Such veteran trees are among the national monuments of Britain. In continental Europe, trees that are more than 200 years old are very scarce, but in Britain they are often a conspicuous feature of old parkland, where they rise above pastures grazed by cattle, sheep and deer. Many survive in parks that now lie in the hearts of cities, while others preside over village greens and ancient churchyards, and are often dignified by their own names.

Pagan survivals

Any tree of any species can become a veteran if it survives beyond the age at which it would normally be felled for timber. However, the maximum age that a tree can reach varies considerably between species. The silver birch, which can survive in exposed conditions and has the ability to colonise open

◄ **Centuries of pollarding, followed by another century or so of neglect, have resulted in the contorted appearance of this ancient beech.**

Trees cover more than 27,300km² (10,500 sq miles) of Britain, and some have survived for more than 200 years. Many of these true veterans feature in local legends.

areas very quickly, rarely lives for more than 80 years, but oak and yew have barely got into their stride by the age of 200 years. Some pedunculate oaks – the common lowland oak of Britain and Ireland – are more than 1000 years old, and some churchyard yews have been alive for at least 2000 years. Some of these may mark pagan sacred sites that predate Christianity.

Extended life

Many veteran trees owe their great age to a management technique called pollarding. This involves removing the limbs of the tree, usually some 2m (6ft) or more from the ground, and allowing the stump to sprout new growth, which can then be harvested a few years later. Pollarding is essentially the same as coppicing, but the tree is cut above head height.

Historically, pollarding was a feature of wooded pasture where animals were grazed beneath the trees. Carried out every 14 years or so, the technique ensured that the tender, edible shoots that

STAG-HEADED TREES

As a tree enters old age, it becomes less productive and invests less energy in its leafy crown, even though it will continue to grow in girth. As the tree takes up fewer nutrients, a certain amount of foliage dies back, and the result is a 'stag-headed' tree. The effect is best seen from a distance, with the dead 'antlers' emerging from the leafy growth beneath.

On the face of it, the tree appears to be dying, but in fact it has simply reduced the size of its crown, leaving the stouter timbers intact. It may survive like this for decades or even centuries.

Ancient oaks often become 'stag-headed' in appearance when nutrients fail to reach the topmost branches. The dead wood attracts timber-boring insects.

sprouted from the stump were out of reach of the animals, protecting future wood crops.

A newly pollarded tree is a sorry sight, but the process often prolongs the tree's life because removing the heavy crown makes the tree less vulnerable to storm damage.

A beech tree, for example, may have a normal lifespan of 250 years, but a pollarded beech may live for 400 years or more.

▶ **Stag beetles need dead wood as food for their larvae. Adult males may look alarming, but they are harmless.**

◀ **Great spotted woodpeckers find plenty of insect prey in the beetle-ridden timber of ancient trees. They also use the trees as nesting sites.**

▼ **Nuthatches use their stout bills to hack away at bark and timber as they search for insects. Their unique habit of climbing down tree trunks head-first makes them instantly identifiable.**

On common land, people had the right to pollard trees for firewood and to graze livestock beneath them. Burnham Beeches in Buckinghamshire is a prime example of such common wood-pasture, containing many fine examples of pollarded beeches that are more than 400 years old. The trees were first cut at the age of 25–35 years and thereafter every 12–15 years.

Pollarding is hard work, and the practice declined as coal became widely available. Most pollards were last cut many decades ago, and the new growth has matured into thick branches that form strange shapes where they sprout from the ancient stumps. This is why many veteran trees look so contorted.

◄ A cavity left where a large branch has fallen makes an ideal roosting site for a tawny owl. The subtle pattern of the owl's soft plumage provides it with almost perfect camouflage.

Parkland oaks

After the Norman Conquest in the 11th century, large tracts of land were set aside as areas where deer were protected. Known as 'forests', initially these were royal preserves, and one of the most famous survives as Windsor Great Park in Berkshire. However, it soon became fashionable for every local lord to enclose land for the purpose of keeping deer. The trees within these parks were either left to their own devices or pollarded and harvested for their wood

Ancient trees growing in parks and hedgerows get plenty of light, encouraging climbers such as traveller's joy to scramble through the open canopy.

every few years. The pollarded trees tended to outlive the others, creating open wood-pastures dotted with veteran trees. Many survived into the 18th century, to catch the eye of landscape architects such as Capability Brown, who valued their majestic beauty. As a result veteran trees still grace many parks today.

Mossy carpet

Ancient trees are an important habitat for lichens and liverworts. One of the most spectacular is the beard lichen, *Usnea subfloridana,* which can be found in the damper parts of the British Isles, mainly in the west, and can completely cover the branches and trunks of its host tree. Such luxuriant lichen growth is a sign of clean air, because lichens do not flourish in areas that suffer from air pollution.

Trees growing in damper areas may also support mosses and ferns. One fern strongly associated with veteran trees is the common polypody, the divided strap-like fronds of which can be seen growing on moss-laden trunks or even high up among the branches, rooted among the mosses and damp debris that accumulate in the craggy bark.

Ancient trees may attract climbing plants. The dark, sinuous growth of ivy often masks the bulk of such trees,

◄ The trunk and spreading branches of this ancient pollarded oak are smothered with lichens, mosses and ferns, which live off the water and nutrients that collect in bark fissures and crevices.

and is wrongly blamed for the apparent ill-health of its hosts. Traveller's joy (wild clematis) and briar roses may festoon the boughs of a veteran tree, investing its ancient limbs with some youthful vigour.

One of the most intriguing plants to be seen growing on veteran trees is the mistletoe. It favours old lime and apple trees, and its bushy growths are at their most conspicuous in winter, when their green vitality makes a vivid contrast with the leafless branches. Its white berries are attractive to a wide range of birds, including the aptly named mistle thrush, but the flesh is very sticky. A feeding bird often finds itself with a berry stuck to its bill, and rids itself of the nuisance by scraping its bill against the rough bark of a tree. This forces the berry into a bark crevice, where the seed within takes root and sprouts into a new mistletoe plant. Although it can make some of its own food, its roots draw sap from its host tree. Mistletoe is therefore a partial parasite, yet despite this it rarely causes any real harm to its host.

Life-giving dead wood

Many veteran trees appear to be half dead, which is a sign of ageing but not necessarily that the whole tree is about to die. The living parts often carry on functioning normally, even if many of the branches have died and the centre of the trunk has rotted away. In some ways, it is just the tree's way of lightening the load.

For wildlife, the importance of dead wood can hardly be overstated. Trapped inside every fragment of dead wood are the chemical building blocks and energy molecules needed by all life. These are consumed by microscopic bacteria and fungi, which give way to a multitude of insects and other invertebrates. More than 1000 British species of invertebrate are associated with this environment.

A close look at any piece of dead wood from an ancient tree will reveal the tunnels of wood-boring beetles. The biggest are made by the larvae of the stag beetle, one of the most spectacular native British insects. It gets its name from the antler-like mandibles of the male, which it uses for

▶ Common polypody fern is one of the most abundant ferns in the British Isles. Sheltered from frosts by the trees, it will retain its colour until December.

▼ Bunches of mistletoe are easy to spot high up in the leafless branches of old trees in winter. The tiny four-petalled flowers develop into sticky white berries that contain the plant's seeds.

▶ Noctule bats use natural tree holes for their daytime roosts, and such sites are common in veteran trees.

display to attract females, and to wrestle with other males. It has a short life as an adult, flying in search of a mate on warm nights in spring and early summer, but as a larva it spends years feeding on dead wood, often in the rotting heart of an ancient tree.

Living larder

Trees with a profusion of dead wood and insect life are literally crawling with food for woodpeckers. Throughout the winter, great spotted woodpeckers can be seen using their long barbed tongues to extract insect grubs from their burrows. Later in the year, the birds use any resonant dead branches as drumming posts, hammering rapidly with their bills to advertise their territorial claims and attract breeding partners. They may also bore nesting cavities in the dead timber.

Immense trunks are typical of veteran oak trees, such as these fine old specimens, which grace Windsor Great Park. They also have relatively sparse crowns.

DEAD WOOD FUNGI

The abundant dead wood on and in a veteran tree is broken down by a variety of fungi. Much of this work goes on unseen. The fruiting bodies of fungi – in the shape of toadstools and bracket fungi – sprout from the wood during certain seasons, often autumn, but the tiny fungal threads that give rise to these spore-carrying structures are ever-present in the timber. They initiate the process of decay by attacking the dead heart of the tree and reducing it to a pulp. This is then colonised by invertebrate animals, such as woodlice. Together they eat out the heart of the ancient trunk, while leaving the surrounding living tissue to create a hollow tree.

▶ Split-gill fungus gets its name from its radiating and branching gills. It often grows on the dead wood of veteran trees, especially ancient beeches. Split-gills are most common in south-east England, and may appear at any time of year when the weather is mild and damp.

Species such as the split-gill, the colourful cinnabar polypore and the often large maze-gill bracket fungus are all to be found within such hollow trees. They may have been active in the trees for centuries, converting the dead wood to dust and

leaving only the outer wood and bark as a living, hollow cylinder. Yet since a broad, hollow cylinder is stronger than a solid trunk of the same weight, many hollow trees survive storms that destroy healthy trees of just half their age.

◀ Sometimes known as chicken-of-the-woods, the sulphur polypore grows in massed tiers of brackets. It usually attacks old oaks, hollowing them out.

▼ The fruiting bodies of southern bracket fungus grow in tiers on the trunks of old trees, releasing many millions of spores that stain the bark below them red.

▲ Dense clusters of branching oyster bracket fungus may appear at the bases of veteran trees in damp weather. In mild years the fungus can be found throughout the winter months.

In winter the bare branches make woodpeckers relatively easy to watch as they feed high in the trees. Nuthatches can also be seen moving jerkily over the branches and trunks of these old trees, searching for insects in the deep recesses of the bark, and occasionally hammering at nuts that they wedge in crevices for the purpose. Nuthatches often breed in old woodpecker nesting holes, but they need to make a few alterations before they can move in. The entrance is always too large, so the female nuthatch reduces

its size by plastering mud around it, to keep out unwelcome visitors.

While the nuthatch works its way up, along and even down a tree – no other British bird descends head-first – the treecreeper has a different, yet equally distinctive feeding style. It creeps up the trunk in a spiralling shuffle, using its long, thin bill to prise tiny insects out of nooks and crannies. When it has climbed well into the crown it flies down to the base of a nearby tree and starts climbing again.

Where a large branch has snapped off, the resulting wound can eventually rot to leave a hole. In a wood, this may make a secure roosting site for a tawny owl, enabling it

to spend the day completely hidden from any small birds that might otherwise harass it. At nightfall it emerges to hunt, using its keen hearing and superb night vision to locate and catch small mammals.

A similar hole in a veteran tree growing in open parkland might harbour a little owl. This stubby owl, with its shocked-looking stare, can often be seen perched on a fence post during the day. It feeds on a wide range of prey, from insects and earthworms to mice, voles and small birds.

Roosting bats
The ragged wounds, loose bark, deep crevices and hollowed-out trunks of ancient trees are important roosting

sites for bats. They provide places for the bats to rest during the day, hibernate in winter and, if large enough, to raise their young in spring.

One species of bat that is largely dependent on veteran trees is the noctule. This large bat feeds mainly on night-flying moths and beetles during the summer, when the females set up their nursery colonies in abandoned woodpecker holes and other sheltered cavities. When the first frosts of autumn occur in October, the bats seek the deepest hollows in ancient trees, where they will be well insulated from hard winter weather. They keep feeding for as long as possible, but become less active as winter gets a grip. Eventually they retreat into full hibernation, allowing body temperature and heart rate to drop to a point that is just enough for survival. They remain like this for the winter, and will not be seen again until the following March.

Another animal that may live in a cavity in a veteran tree is the honeybee. Most honeybees live in artificial hives, but wild colonies often make their home in hollow trees or in hollowed-out branches. The insulation provided by the timber – plus the bees' stored supply of honey – enables the colony to survive through the winter until flower nectar becomes available in early spring.

Ancient landmarks

Unsurprisingly, veteran trees have become woven into the fabric of local history, custom and legend. Many are mentioned in old records, and have a role in traditional festivals. Some even have a legal significance, because in the years before accurate maps, parish boundaries were defined by lists of lines drawn – or walked, in a ritual circuit known as perambulation – between physical features that often included trees.

Despite this, veteran trees are frequently the victims of misguided management. To

some people, a gnarled, hollow, stag-headed tree is a neglected eyesore, fit only for firewood. Local authorities often feel impelled to lop the dead branches from ancient trees in public places, on the grounds that they could fall and injure someone. Such

action can easily lead to the destruction of a tree – from the tree surgeon's view, it is completely unsound. Fortunately, many of the veteran trees that survive on private parkland are left to manage themselves, and most of them will outlive us all.

In many ways, veteran trees such as this ancient alder are best appreciated during the winter months, when the leaves that mask their contorted shapes have fallen away.

Few trees can be as steeped in legend as the Major Oak of Sherwood Forest. Its vast trunk is topped with the gnarled growth of ancient pollarding.

WILDLIFE WATCH

Where can I see veteran trees?

● Windsor Great Park, Berkshire, is still a forest in the truest sense. Owned by Crown Estates, it has many fine specimens of veteran trees.

● Burnham Beeches, Buckinghamshire, is owned by the Corporation of London. This ancient wood-pasture contains fine pollarded beeches on traditional common land.

● The New Forest, Hampshire, is now a National Park. This old hunting forest is dominated by oak, beech and heath, with many veteran trees in the ancient woodland.

● Sherwood Forest, Nottinghamshire, has ancient oaks that still survive in the woodland near Ollerton.

● Look in city parks and stately homes with extensive grounds. Many of them still have veteran trees that are centuries old.

● Many old churchyards have ancient yews that are more than a thousand years old, and some are living survivors from prehistory.

A year in the life of the Eden Project

In the depths of Cornwall, a disused china clay pit has been transformed into an enchanting paradise. Beneath huge domed conservatories and among terraced gardens lies the most ambitious staging of plantlife ever attempted in Britain.

Set in a crater 60m (200ft) deep, Eden's giant domes face south towards the sea. The Project took nearly four years to build and is being constantly extended.

In the morning light of early winter the Cornish countryside is splashed with colour. A rich patchwork of heathers, bracken and gorse, punctuated by the reds of hedgerow berries, illustrates that here the end of the year is not necessarily a time of death or decay. With the sun barely an hour above the horizon, the air is crisp and carries with it the moist, salty tang of the sea that lies just a few kilometres to the south. Influenced by the Gulf Stream, this balmy climate enables a wide variety of plants to flourish in England's westernmost county.

On arrival at Eden, a dense twiggy tangle of hawthorn and hazel hedges screens the view until the last moment, when all at once the spectacle opens out. Inevitably, the steel webs of the two massive domed conservatories command attention. In a landscape almost completely devoid of straight lines, the eight interconnected bubbles that form the domes look both alien and yet surprisingly at home in the huge crater in which they are located.

Nature in winter

Neither a green theme park nor a botanical garden in the traditional sense, even in the depths of winter the Eden Project has much to see. In the words of chief executive Tim Smit, the intention was to 'create a global garden where people can appreciate the wealth of nature'. To achieve this, Eden presents more than 80 managed displays of more than 4000 plant species – in all around 80,000 plants – from the world's three major 'biomes', or naturally occurring plant communities from a particular habitat or climatic region. Two of these, the humid tropics biome and the warm temperate biome, are housed within the domes. The largest biome of all is the cool temperate biome – also referred to as the outdoor biome – which covers an area of 10 hectares (25 acres). Many of the plants are initially nurtured at the Watering Lane Nursery, situated just five miles away, which is owned by the Project.

The young fronds of the soft tree fern, a native of the temperate rainforest of south-east Australia, uncurl as they grow.

The winter months are perhaps the best time of year to appreciate the way in which Eden has been designed. From the rim of the pit, there are wonderful views of the beautifully curved terraces that arc around the Project's centre in sweeps, each one laid out in such a way that the plants create a living tapestry. Surprises aplenty are in store, with traditional Cornish crops, such as cauliflowers and purple-sprouting broccoli, growing beside rows of tea plants, *Camellia sinensis*, which in turn are near the hop plants that are used to flavour beer.

Although the winter scene is largely painted in hues of brown and green, over a million bulbs have been planted around the whole site and by December the first daffodil buds are opening to illuminate the panorama with flashes of yellow. Evergreens are also noticeable at this time of year. Descending from the rim of the crater down a steep, winding path known as the zigzag, plants that have been well established on Earth since before the

Plantings of summer vegetables are a feature of Eden's outdoor biome, which takes advantage of Cornwall's mild climate.

dinosaurs can be seen. These are the ferns – flowerless plants that reproduce from spores. Among the largest of these, the Australian soft tree fern, *Dicksonia antarctica*, can reach a height of 9m (30ft) with fronds up to 4.5m (15ft) in length. Grown today as an exotic ornamental, to the indigenous people of Australia it once represented a valuable source of food. The pith in the upper part of the trunk can be eaten raw or roasted and is highly

CREATING AN ECOSYSTEM FROM SCRATCH

The Eden Project finally opened in March 2001, based on an idea first mooted just six years earlier. As well as showing the fabulous span of the world of plants, its aim was to show how plants underpin every aspect of life on Earth, providing everything from cleaner air to food, clothing, fuel, shelter and medicine.

In May 1997, the Eden Project's bid for funding was accepted by the Millennium Commission and £37 million awarded. A little over a year later the task of building Eden began in a disused china clay pit at Bodelva, near St Austell in Cornwall. Turning the vast, sterile crater into a lush celebration of the world's plantlife involved raising the floor of the pit by 20m (66ft), lowering the rim by 13m (45ft) and tidying up the 1.8 million tonnes of spoil that littered the whole area.

The site contained virtually no soil and in order to carpet the pit to an acceptable depth for planting, 85,000 tonnes were needed. To take this amount of topsoil from somewhere else was not only too expensive but also ecologically unethical. Instead, another abandoned clay pit was requisitioned and the Eden team set about making their own. Soil takes many years to form naturally but the team had just two years. Working with experts from the University of Reading, inorganic spoil from the clay extraction process – mostly sand – was combined with huge amounts of composted waste and mixed together by big JCBs. Not only was this 'home-made' soil environmentally friendly, it was also disease and pest free. Even better, it could be mixed to suit the many different plants that would soon populate the site.

Each of the heated biomes comprises four separate domes that imitate the structure of soap bubbles. Their exact positioning was worked out so that they receive the maximum amount of sunlight throughout the year. To help reduce energy requirements, the domes rest against a granite rock face that absorbs heat during the day and releases it at night, like a giant storage heater.

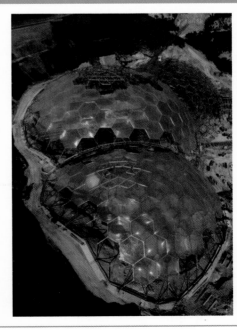

The domes are constructed from hexagons of tubular steel covered in a transparent, recyclable film, and are guaranteed to be maintenance-free for at least 25 years.

nutritious, while the young leaves reputedly taste like bitter celery.

Following a stroll around to the west of the site, a group of spiky Central American plants with very different uses are encountered – the agaves. From *Agave americana*, for example, tequila is distilled. Eden has one of the largest examples of this plant in Britain, standing over 3m (10ft) tall and 3m (10ft) wide. Much less imposing, but equally valuable, is *Agave sisalana*, the plant from which sisal rope and matting are made. When so much cordage for boats and ships is synthetic, produced from non-renewable resources, it's easy to forget that everything from garden twine to a ship's anchor rope can still be made from plants.

Although during the winter months many of the trees are bare, they can often be identified from their silhouettes – the tall upward-swept branches of the poplar are unmistakable. Many other native trees are grown here. The open, spreading beech is familiar as is the willow, which is one of the most versatile of trees. Not only does its bark

▶ **Early blooming daffodils grown in Cornwall were once sold in flower markets throughout the country.**

▼ **Most of the world's natural sisal fibre is made from the large fleshy leaves of *Agave sisalana*. Each rosette can grow to around 2m (6ft) tall.**

contain salicylic acid – the source of aspirin – but its wood has traditionally been used to make everything from hurdles to cricket bats. Ash and hazel grow here, as well as many naturalised species, such as horse chestnut.

New growth

Spring comes early to Cornwall and winter daffodils are soon joined by a riotous host of hyacinths, tulips and narcissi. From March to May, Eden presents a 'Bulb Mania' festival, staged by experts from Cornwall and Holland.

New life is also stirring in the vegetable garden, the so-called 'plants for taste'. Freshly planted each February and March, by late spring the vegetable plots are flush with early lettuce, chard, onions and leeks, as well as sprawling Turk's turban gourds and purple spheres of kohlrabi.

▲ **A perennial, sweetly aromatic herb with narrow, greyish green leaves, lavender needs well-drained soil and plenty of sun. It thrives in these conditions at Eden.**

◀ **Sunflowers always turn to face the sun. Their impressive flowerheads can grow up to 30cm (12in) across and they often reach 3m (10ft) tall.**

Although the odd cabbage white butterfly can be seen fluttering around the leaves, the mixed planting helps diminish the impact of these and other pest species, as perhaps does the companion planting of marigolds and nasturtiums. Their flowers attract predatory insects, such as wasps and hoverflies, which eat caterpillars and aphids. The yellow and gold of the flowers blooming among the vegetables makes an eye-catching sight.

Pests are not especially prevalent at Eden, because of these measures, but for those that do become troublesome, organic remedies are sought. Slugs for example, can be a perennial problem so these

are controlled with applications of tiny parasitic nematode worms, which attack the young slugs. When aphid populations outstrip the ability of natural predators to control them, soap sprays are used that cause minimal damage to the plants.

Using plants in industry

A short walk from the vegetable garden is an exhibit of 'plants for tomorrow's industries'. By late spring visitors can almost find their way there blindfolded, simply by following the scent of lavender. Not only a valuable source of perfume, lavender also has antiseptic qualities. Scentless, but visually as stunning, are rows and rows of sunflowers. Long used as a cooking oil, the sunflower's potential as a substitute engine oil is now being realised. In fact, all the machinery at Eden is lubricated with plant-based oil. Even more surprising to discover is that the maize flourishing nearby has not escaped from Eden's vegetable garden but is being grown to highlight its increasing use as a source of plastic. Plastic from maize is already being used to make disposable cutlery and biodegradable cutlery is used as mulch around the plants.

HUGE HOTHOUSES

Undoubtedly, the great, covered biomes constitute the heart of the Eden Project. The larger of the two, the humid tropics biome, showcases plantlife from four key areas – tropical islands, Malaysia, South America and Africa. Within this hot, sticky jungle, with temperatures ranging between 19°C (66°F) and 35°C (95°F) and a humidity of up to 90 per cent, more than 1000 different plant species thrive. For instance, balsa and kapok trees that can shoot up 3m (10ft) a year are already reaching the roof, while below them tropical bamboos are increasing in height by up to 45cm (18in) a day.

Among the rare species are the Coco-de-Mer and the white-flowered Busy Lizzie, *Impatiens gordonii*, both from the Seychelles. For many visitors, however, everyday species have more impact than rare plants. For instance, cola trees, from which soft drinks are made, coco trees, the source of all things chocolate, and the sapodilla tree, from which comes chewing gum, bear their fruits here for all to see and sometimes even taste.

The warm temperate biome features plants from the Mediterranean, South Africa and California with their hot dry summers and cool wet winters. The air is drier and temperatures range from 18–30°C (46–86°F) in summer, 9–18°C (48–64°F) in winter. Unlike the fast-growing plants of the humid tropics, those of the temperate zone are both slow growing and compact, so this biome has taken longer to become established. However, a visit in spring or summer will be rewarded by a breathtaking display of flowers, including a collection of tulips. Most exotic, though, is

the bird of paradise plant, *Strelitzia reginae*, from South Africa, which can grow up to 1.2m (4ft) tall.

Rambling vines and cork oaks, *Quercus suber*, accompany another favourite from the Mediterranean region, the olive. Some old, gnarled trees, long past their productive best, have been brought from Sicily to grow alongside smaller younger trees. They have been planted in threes, in the way they were traditionally grown in Spain.

▲ Plants of the tropical rainforest, such as palms and tree ferns, grow constantly and quickly in the controlled climate of the humid tropics biome.

▼ In the warm temperate biome, humidity is kept down by using a system of vents. Fungal infections may otherwise attack leaves of plants such as these aloes.

▲ Tree frogs have been released in the humid tropics biome to keep the higher levels of the canopy insect free.

▲ The huge seeds of the Coco-de-Mer can weigh up to 18kg (38lb) and take seven years to ripen. It is a protected species.

▶ Stunning orange or purple flowers offset the subtle greyish green foliage of the bird of paradise plant.

Eden's many steep banks present enormous challenges to the Project's gardeners. Laying coir matting and planting the slopes to establish a network of roots are two proven ways of stabilising the soil. At the Project, willow is often used for this purpose while, in the least accessible areas, grass and wildflower seed mixes have been hydroblasted onto the slopes using high-pressure hoses. A more unusual choice of plant for this function is the climbing hydrangea, *Hydrangea seemannii*. Although Mexican in origin, it seems to enjoy the Cornish air so much that it has rapidly climbed over many of the more precipitous slopes, clothing them in its shiny, leathery leaves. By late June, these banks are awash with sprays of ivory white hydrangea flowers, which attract butterflies, such as the red admiral and small tortoiseshell.

Cornish restoration

Tucked away on the far western fringes of the site, two areas are devoted to traditional Cornish habitats, Atlantic woodland and lowland heath. Both were once widespread in the county but today are significantly diminished.

Atlantic woodland, consisting of sessile oak, willow, ash and hazel trees, often swathed in ferns and mosses, was once predominant in the south-west. Sessile oaks, *Quercus petraea*, were the first trees to be planted in the outdoor biome and, although still nearly half a century away from maturity, by late summer a few acorns can be seen. The sessile oak is one of Britain's two native oak species. In common with its cousin, the English or pedunculate oak, it is valuable because such oaks play host to a wealth of other wildlife when they mature. To help encourage the re-establishment of oak trees, one of the Eden Project's partners, English Nature, is recreating up to 1000 hectares (2500 acres) of woodland in the Cornish clay countryside around Eden, restoring a habitat that has been almost lost for a century.

Lowland heath, as its name suggests, is dominated by bell heather, cross-leaved heath and, in Cornwall, the rare Cornish heath *Erica vagans*. Since 1945 Cornwall has lost more than three-fifths of its lowland heath but restoration of this habitat throughout the county has now begun.

▲ Cornwall's long flowering season means that in late summer, banks of colour still greet visitors to the outdoor biome.

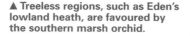

▲ Treeless regions, such as Eden's lowland heath, are favoured by the southern marsh orchid.

◀ Tiny, star-shaped flowers of heath bedstraw, one of the commonest moorland plants, dot Eden's burgeoning wild Cornwall site.

▲ The bell-shaped flowers of foxgloves hang from a single stem, always on the same side.

At Eden, though, the wild Cornwall area is not just a shrine to rare species – it also celebrates the familiar. On the steep slopes in summer, flamboyant sprays of purple foxgloves, *Digitalis purpurea*, abound together with the delicate, sweetly scented white flowers of heath bedstraw, *Galium saxatile*. Perhaps most exciting of all, however, is to find the delightfully intricate reddish lilac blooms of the southern marsh orchid, *Dactylorhiza praetermissa*. These lovely little flowers were not planted but found their own way to Eden.

Every year more than a million people visit the Eden Project and most leave impressed by what they have seen. Within the once-barren clay pit a special magic has been wrought that is achieving the founder's original aim of putting plants back where they belong – centre stage.

Places to visit at the Eden Project

An incomparable collection of plants makes the Eden Project well worth a visit at any time of year. Its landscape is constantly changing as plants mature and new ones are added. Eden hosts a wide variety of daytime events, linked to various plant displays, and in the evening stages musical and theatrical performances.

1 Humid tropic biome
The steamy jungle of the tropical rainforest is reproduced in this biome, which is in effect the world's largest greenhouse. Visitors can walk among bamboos and bananas, past crashing waterfalls, and follow the trails that lead high above the lush canopy of trees.

2 Warm temperate biome
The resinous scents of the Mediterranean greet visitors to this warm world, which houses a fascinating collection of plants grown for perfume and cut-flower displays as well as a section of leafy tobacco plants.

3 Outdoor biome
Beautifully landscaped terraces support a wide variety of plants. Hidden among them are many fascinating sculptures and exhibits, such as the amusingly ironic 'Industrial plant' and George Fairfax's towering metal giant in the rope and fibre display.

4 The Link
The entry point for both indoor biomes is located here. A restaurant and café offer a wide selection of food and snacks. Unusually, the building has a grass roof.

5 The Stage
This is the setting for lectures, film shows and the highly popular Eden Sessions, featuring world famous musicians. In July 2005, it hosted Eden's contribution to the Live8 festival. From autumn all through the winter, an ice-skating rink is set up here.

6 Education Centre
Opened in the summer of 2005, the education centre houses a variety of exhibitions and displays that describe the role of plants in the world.

7 Visitor Centre
The entrance to Eden is via the visitor centre, which houses the information desk as well as shops, a café and a restaurant.

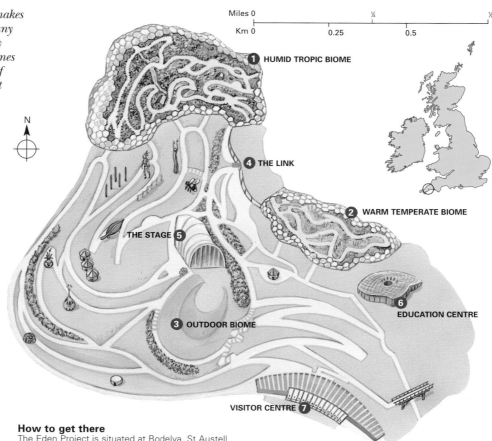

Miles 0 ¼ ½
Km 0 0.25 0.5

1 HUMID TROPIC BIOME

4 THE LINK

2 WARM TEMPERATE BIOME

THE STAGE 5

6 EDUCATION CENTRE

3 OUTDOOR BIOME

VISITOR CENTRE 7

N

How to get there
The Eden Project is situated at Bodelva, St Austell, Cornwall, PL24 2SG. For travellers by car it is signposted from the A30, A390 and A391. For train travellers the nearest station is St Austell. A combined train, bus transfer and admission ticket is available. Telephone 08457 484950 for details. Buses run daily from St Austell, Newquay, Helston, Falmouth and Truro. For more information, telephone the bus company, Truronian, on 01872 273453. The Eden Project is also on the National Cycle Network (visit www.sustrans.org.uk) and discounts are available for those who walk or cycle to the site.

Opening times
Eden is open every day of the year except Christmas Eve and Christmas Day. From 21 March to 31 October the gates open at 9.30am and last entry is at 4.30pm. From 1 November to 20 March the gates open at 10am and the last entry is at 3pm. For further information, telephone 01726 811911 or visit www.edenproject.com

Entry fees
Reduced rates apply for senior citizens, students and children. Under fives are admitted free of charge. Family tickets, group discounts and an annual 'passport' are available, and special guided tours can be booked in advance. Check the website for details.

Banks of monbretia, a semi-hardy member of the iris family, provide a backdrop for the many events staged by Eden throughout the summer.

WILDLIFE WATCH

When is the best time to visit the Eden Project?

● To avoid the crowds it is best to arrive either early or after 2pm. A typical visit usually lasts from two to four hours, and during that time expect to do quite a bit of walking. Wear comfortable shoes and layered clothing to allow for the contrast between the temperature outdoors and the temperature inside the biomes. It's also worth remembering that the domes offer no protection from UV light, so on sunny days it is advisable to wear a sunscreen.

Animals and plants in focus

Garden watch

- The fox
- Hibernating mammals
- The robin
- The blue tit
- The dunnock
- The devil's coach horse
- Lacewings
- Winter garden moths
- Winter garden shrubs
- The holly tree

The fox

Adept at survival, the fox thrives in both city and countryside. In the middle of winter, a vixen's unmistakable screams can sometimes be heard, shattering the quiet of the night as she calls to her mate.

Foxes are to be found the length and breadth of the country, from the centre of London to high up in the Cairngorms of Scotland. Successful predators and effective scavengers, they eat an extraordinarily wide range of food, including rabbits, chickens, fish, beetles, earthworms and even fruit, such as strawberries. This is one reason why, despite sustained campaigns against it, this truly remarkable animal has been able to survive and prosper in increasingly difficult circumstances.

The real secret of the fox's success lies in its adaptability. Not being particularly specialised in its needs means that the fox is able to find food and shelter in most environments. This may be why it seems to be most abundant in places where a mixture of woods, hedgerows, fields and water exists, each providing different opportunities to feed, to lie up and to breed, and all offering an alternative if one place becomes inadequate for some reason. Only a very adaptable animal could take full advantage of such diversity.

Foxes often lie up in dense undergrowth or shelter under a farm outbuilding, a garden shed or a fallen tree. They may use crevices in rocky areas, or old drains, or take over part of a badger sett or rabbit warren. They quite often take up residence in buildings – both empty and occupied – but often dig their own burrows (called earths or dens), especially in dry sandy soils. An earth may have a single entrance but up to four are not unusual. Some large earths may have interconnecting burrows rather than a single tunnel and can have up to a dozen entrances. An earth is marked with a strong and distinctive odour when in use.

A thick winter coat helps the fox to maintain its body temperature and survive the harshest of weather.

Foxes generally prefer to live above ground and use their dens mainly for breeding, although they tend to take sanctuary in them during wet or cold weather. On warm summer nights they will come out even in the rain because warm, wet conditions are ideal for finding worms at the surface. Most of their activity is at night, but foxes will often emerge in the evenings and even in broad daylight in places where they feel safe.

Midwinter crying
The male dog fox and female vixen look similar, but males are usually slightly larger and there are minor differences in the shape of the head.

FOX FACT FILE

Superficially, the fox resembles a dog, but the tail is much thicker and always carried low. In winter, dense fur makes the fox look stout, with short thick legs.

● NAMES
Common names: fox, red fox
Scientific name: *Vulpes vulpes*

● HABITAT
Almost everywhere, from fields to mountains, farms to woodland, sand dunes to city centres

● DISTRIBUTION
Throughout Britain and Ireland, except the Isle of Man and some Scottish islands

● STATUS
Probably more than 250,000 and may be increasing; often regarded as a pest

● SIZE
Body 60–70cm (2ft–2ft 4in), tail 40cm (16in); adult body weight male 6–7kg (13¼–15½lb); female 10% smaller

● KEY FEATURES
Orange-brown body, white throat, long bushy tail that often has a white tip; prominent ears 9cm (3½in) long, with black outer surface

● HABITS
Normally lives alone or in small family group

● VOICE
Loud screaming, mainly by vixen, especially in the breeding season; triple bark, mostly by dog fox, plus a great variety of other noises

● FOOD
Rabbits, mice and other small mammals, birds, earthworms and beetles; also scavenged carcasses, fruit, fish, eggs and a large range of other foods

● BREEDING
Mate from late December to early February; 4–5 young born in March

● EARTH
Uses existing burrows but often digs its own; may make a temporary nest on the surface or live under a garden shed or below the floorboards of a house

● YOUNG
Born covered with dark, chocolate-brown, velvety fur, blind and deaf – eyes open at 11–14 days, milky looking at first, blue until 1 month old; juveniles are similar to adults, but have less bushy tails

When directed forwards, the large ears focus on tiny sounds, helping the fox to locate prey from its movements.

● SIGNS
'Earth' entrance holes about 20cm (8in) in diameter, but long-established ones are much larger with a fan of dug-out soil in front; grey twisted droppings containing fur and bone fragments; very distinctive fox smell, pungent and acrid – quite different from that of a dog – can often be smelt on the wind, around burrows or near food and droppings

▲ Cubs are usually born in an earth in the country. However, any secure cavity may make a good den, including big drain pipes, hollow logs, tree stumps or under buildings.

◄ By the time they start to appear at the entrance to the earth, at about a month old, fox cubs are beginning to look like their parents.

Distribution map key

█ Present all year round

☐ Not present

The thick and bushy tail has a small scent gland on the upper side, but the musty, foxy smell comes mainly from big glands located under the base of the tail.

Extremely sensitive, the nose is used to detect prey and enemies, to locate and follow other foxes – including mates – and also to find previously stored food.

Strong legs enable the fox to trot for long periods without tiring. It can also run fast, jump and climb.

THE URBAN FOX

The fox has adapted well to the urban environment. Living in close proximity has had no obvious ill effects on either foxes or humans.

Foxes can be found living in most towns and cities from the Midlands southwards. In northern England and Wales they are scarcer, while in Scotland, both Edinburgh and parts of Glasgow have thriving populations, as do some Irish cities.

They are most likely to be seen in suburban districts built in the 1920s and 1930s, where the houses have sizeable mature gardens. A typical urban fox territory covers between 20 and 40 hectares (50 to 100 acres) of gardens attached to semi-detached houses, and allotments. The smallest territory ever recorded was just 9 hectares (22 acres), in Bristol.

Foxes come out to hunt after dark, preferring gardens that are not too tidy and offer plenty of bushes for shelter. They concentrate on a relatively small area, probably covering only about 0.5km^2 (¼ sq mile). They look mostly for scraps – crusts of bread or bacon fat left on a bird table make easy pickings for the urban fox, and a plastic bag of leftovers put out by dustbins may be ripped open for food. They also eat worms and windfall fruit, but sometimes take pet guinea pigs or rabbits, too. They take no notice of domestic cats.

Urban foxes can sometimes be watched going about their business in the day, seemingly unconcerned by the presence of humans, but generally they rest while it's light – perhaps on a sun-warmed asphalt roof or a sheltered, hidden patch of grass. During the breeding season, the urban vixen's favourite spot for making a den is the space beneath a garden shed or other outbuilding.

An accomplished scavenger, the fox is not averse to raiding a garden bird table, as well as any available dustbins.

Learning through play

Fox cubs are fully weaned at around ten weeks old but they remain dependent on their parents for several more months. They spend the summer playing, but by the time winter arrives young foxes must be ready to fend for themselves.

Hungry cubs beg for food by nuzzling, licking and even biting their mother's nose. The vixen will soon be teaching these youngsters to fend for themselves.

When a youngster signals submission during a play fight, its playmate would be wise to be wary as it may be a ploy to gain an advantage.

HOW MANY FOXES?

The total fox population in Britain is hard to quantify, but experts think that there are probably at least a quarter of a million, with some 25 per cent living in urban areas. They produce around 500,000 cubs each spring, many of which do not survive. Until the ban on fox-hunting, which came into effect in 2005, various hunts protected cubs, and even deliberately introduced foxes into new areas. Numbers are steadily growing in some parts of Britain, with gamekeepers in the south-east killing seven times as many foxes in 1990 as they did 30 years earlier.

▶ Play fights are vigorous and involve wide open mouths and bared teeth. They rarely last more than a few seconds but are important in teaching young foxes to cope with real aggression when they are older.

▼ These fox cubs are eagerly awaiting the return of one of their parents, bringing food back to the den for them to eat or to play with.

The breeding season lasts from December to February, during which time the dog fox will remain near to a vixen that is ready to breed, following her closely all the time. This is the time of year when foxes are most vocal, males calling at night with three or four-note barks, and vixens with blood-curdling screams.

The social arrangements of foxes vary according to where they are living. Territory sizes can range from 20 hectares (50 acres) or so in urban areas, to as much as 1600 hectares (4000 acres) in the Scottish hills. Foxes may live alone, in pairs or in family groups. When individuals are old enough to leave the group, how far they go depends on how many foxes are living in the area – the fewer the foxes, the larger each pair's or group's territory and the farther the foxes will need to disperse. Territories may overlap but only core areas are used frequently. Some parts of a territory may be rarely visited by the territory owners, or used merely to get from one place to another.

Foxes mark territories by squirting urine on to fences, tree trunks and other solid objects at nose height for the information of the next fox that passes by. Faeces also form territorial markers. Interestingly, marking behaviour is least frequent at territory boundaries but is used right across the area that the fox usually inhabits, and especially along regularly used paths. This means the whole territory is marked, not just its edges. Research has found that dominant individuals leave scent marks no more frequently than subordinates.

Leaving home

When they are about six months old, some of the juveniles begin to move away from the family group. Around three-quarters of male cubs leave their home territory by the time they are a year old, but only about a third of females do so. In large families, the smallest animals are the most likely to leave, either walking non-stop or making a series of short journeys spread over several days or weeks. Few things get in their way in the search for a new home, and foxes have been known to cross rivers and even tidal mudflats. Males go farther than females, sometimes up to 50km (30 miles).

The females that do not leave their home area remain as part of the family group. As many as six additional young females may assist with bringing up the cubs of the dominant female in the following year. These 'helpers' guard, groom and play with the young and retrieve them if they stray.

Females are capable of breeding for the first time when they are 10 months old, and their family will then be born around the time of the vixen's own first birthday. However, not all females will breed successfully this early in their lives, and many do not do so until their second year.

Art of communication

Foxes use a wide variety of facial expressions to convey their moods to each other, just as dogs and people do. Even young cubs do this, making open-mouthed threat gestures towards each other when annoyed.

A variety of body postures indicates either aggressive intent or submission, and foxes also have a great number of calls at their disposal. These vary from the yelping and whining of the cubs to the barks and screams of the adults. One researcher distinguished 40 basic types of sound grouped into 28 different calls. All this helps the animals to communicate

CATCHING MICE

Mice and voles generally move along narrow runways through grass and other vegetation, where it is hard for the fox to follow. Having located an unwary mouse by the slight noises it makes or by sight, or both, the fox leaps in the air, landing on top of it and using its paws and mouth to trap the prey.

With ears facing forwards and eyes fixed intently on the source of tiny sounds, a fox jumps on its prey.

with, and to understand, each other, and to react towards each other in the most appropriate manner. When provoked, two foxes will rear up on their hind legs and paw at each other, with mouths wide open. Real aggression is rare, however. Just occasionally a fox will kill its opponent but death and serious injuries are infrequent.

Hunting techniques

Strategies vary according to circumstances. Sometimes foxes stalk prey, rushing up to grab it at the last moment. Other times they creep quietly through long grass to pounce on small mammals.

Hunting for earthworms involves trotting rapidly back and forth over areas of short grass on warm moist nights, searching for worms lying on the surface. A keen sense of hearing enables the fox to detect worms by any slight noises they make as they move. Earthworms form a large part of the diet of urban foxes and of those living in semi-rural areas, but country foxes eat relatively few of them.

Generally speaking, foxes do not attack or kill many lambs, but often eat dead ones. They eat other carrion too, including deer and scavenged road victims, biting the feathers off pigeons and other large birds before eating the body.

Foxes raid nesting seabird colonies whenever they get the chance, especially those of gulls and terns, and in places, severely reduce the breeding success of ducks, partridges and pheasants by attacking females that are incubating eggs. They can eat whole clutches and may be responsible for around one third of all pheasant eggs lost to predators.

Occasionally, a fox will kill chickens, or sometimes wild birds, far in excess of the amount needed for food in order to stimulate its attacking instinct. This is called 'surplus killing'. In some gull colonies, more than 200 birds have been killed in a single night. In a chicken coop, from which the birds cannot usually escape, the fox may lose control in the pandemonium and rush about killing frightened birds for as long as any remain alive. At other times, surplus food may be hidden away – often partially buried – to be retrieved when needed.

Changing coat

From about Easter time, the winter coat moults and foxes look very moth-eaten, but by midsummer all the old fur has been replaced with a sleek, shorter coat. In autumn, additional hair grows and the thickening of the underfur gives the animal its chunky winter profile.

When numbers are high, foxes may suffer from outbreaks of mange, which is caused by scabies mites. Millions of mites build up in the skin, starting at the tail, where hair falls out first. The intense irritation causes constant scratching and the fox sheds its fur. It may lose over half its body weight before dying after some three to four months of misery. Over the last 10 to 15 years, there has been a big increase in the incidence of mange in both urban and rural foxes. In one severe outbreak, in Bristol in 1994, the fox population was reduced by a 95 per cent in just two years.

High mortality

Male foxes seem to live longer than females, occasionally reaching 10 years or more, but around one year is more usual and few survive more than two years. Foxes that leave the area where they were born tend to have a reduced life expectancy, partly because of the hazards

Run, rabbit, run!

The fox's method of hunting a rabbit is to select one that seems less wary than the others. This may not necessarily be the nearest, but the one that offers the best chance of success.

The fox keeps low and begins to creep towards its prey.

Other rabbits stand their ground as the fox rushes forward, glancing up to confirm that the rabbit is still vulnerable to attack.

◄ In autumn and winter, as establishing territory and mating become important, and finding food becomes harder, fights can be serious and sometimes very fierce.

WILDLIFE WATCH

Where can I see foxes?

● Foxes are more likely to be seen in towns and cities than in the country.

● At dusk and after dark, foxes come out in search of food, especially in parks and gardens and on waste ground.

● In safe, quiet places, they may be seen basking in the sunshine.

● Foxes often inhabit railway embankments and may be seen from trains.

that they encounter during their search for a new home. Many die on the roads and it is thought that about 100,000 are killed each year by gamekeepers and others. Foxes often die from poisoning, either through eating illegally set baits, or prey or carrion that has itself been poisoned, sometimes by agricultural chemicals such as insecticides.

Other causes of death include being killed by predators – dogs and birds of prey sometimes kill cubs. Fox hunts (banned in 2005) used to kill about 12,500 a year. Twice that number are destroyed by forestry workers and fox eradication teams. This high mortality rate means that pairs of foxes are unlikely to survive very long and the remaining animal must find a new mate. Despite all this, the fox seems to be holding its own or modestly increasing in numbers.

► Cubs learn how to tackle prey by practising on dead animals brought by their parents. At first, though, even picking up a meal can prove to be a challenge.

The fox lowers its head again to make its final headlong dash towards the selected rabbit.

The fox pounces on its prey, trapping it with all four paws against the ground while the jaws get a strong and deadly grip.

Finally, the fox breaks the rabbit's neck by biting deeply or shaking the animal violently while holding it by the head.

Hibernating mammals

While many garden birds escape the food shortages of winter by flying to warmer places, a few mammals adopt a more radical strategy. They save energy by spending the winter months in the deep sleep of hibernation.

When temperatures begin to drop below freezing on late autumn nights, small animals such as insects and earthworms start to disappear. Many adult insects are killed off by the frost, and the larvae that survive them often slip into sheltered crevices to weather the winter. Others burrow deep underground, along with the earthworms. Either way, the larger animals that rely on them for food are left with a problem. They cannot find enough to eat.

Mammals – and birds – need a lot of energy. They need it not just for activity, but to fuel their bodily functions and to maintain the constant high body temperature that is characteristic of warm-blooded animals. They obtain this energy from their food, so if they cannot locate enough food, they find it more and more difficult to balance their 'energy budget'. They could easily burn more energy looking for food than they obtain

from digesting the few items that they do find. Moreover, with falling temperatures, especially at night, the amount of energy that they need to keep their bodies warm increases. At some point, searching for food is no longer a viable option.

Slowing down

Some animals deal with the problem by migration – they go to live in places where they can still find enough food. Many insect-eating birds do this, with garden species such as swifts, house martins and flycatchers travelling as far as tropical Africa for the winter. However, this is not an option for hedgehogs and dormice, which must stay put. They have to find another way of coping.

Their solution is to opt out of the most energy-expensive activities, such as moving about and maintaining a high body temperature. Instead, an animal such as a dormouse slips into a state of

dormancy that allows its temperature to fall until it is virtually the same as that of the environment. This means that, amazingly, the dormouse's body temperature may be only a degree or two above freezing. If the environmental temperature falls much lower than this, its metabolism switches on at a low level to raise its blood temperature just high enough to prevent freezing and frostbite.

Effectively, the dormouse gives up being warm-blooded, as well as all activity. This saves over 90 per cent of its normal daily energy expenditure, and enables it to tick over in a state of suspended animation until the spring. This is true hibernation.

The hazel dormouse makes a winter nest from tightly woven shredded plant material. It lies rolled up inside, with its tail curled over its body. Even if it is disturbed, it remains rolled up and incapable of rapid movement for some time – at least 20 minutes – before waking up.

FATTENING UP

British hibernators do not store food in their winter nests. During hibernation, the small amount of energy needed to keep the animal's metabolism just ticking over is supplied by using up white fat stored under the skin and around the intestines. Very large amounts of fat are needed to sustain five or six months of hibernation.

Fat is laid down in autumn, when food is plentiful. Like money in a bank, it is drawn upon as needed over winter. About one third of the animal's weight is lost as these fat reserves are consumed, and if there is insufficient fat to last the winter, the animal will die before spring arrives.

In order to survive the winter, a hedgehog needs to build up its weight to at least 450g (16oz) before it hibernates, otherwise it will run out of energy and die in about February or March. Similarly, a common or hazel dormouse needs to weigh 12–15g (½oz), or it will not have enough fat to keep it going through the long winter months.

▲ Fat dormice gorge on hazel nuts, beech mast and acorns in the autumn. They will not feed again for at least five months, and may hibernate for more than half the year. In some years they enter hibernation as early as August, and they are rarely seen before May.

◄ Young hazel dormice feed intensively in the autumn in order to build up their fat reserves before hibernation. By eating energy-rich hazel nuts and similar autumn foods they can double their weight in just a week or two.

Low temperatures

A mammal's body is like a machine that operates properly only within a certain temperature range, averaging 37°C (98.6°F). If its body temperature falls below this range, as it does during hibernation, many metabolic processes no longer take place at the normal speed. Digestion ceases and breathing slows to just a few breaths per minute, usually in brief bursts rather than continuously. A hibernating hedgehog averages 13 breaths per minute. Meanwhile, its heart rate, which usually exceeds 100 beats per minute, slows to some five beats per minute. The blood circulates very sluggishly and its chemical composition changes. More changes occur in the liver and other internal organs.

Muscles will not work normally at such low body temperatures, so the animal is capable of only very slow movements. It is stiff, cold and seems almost dead. This inert state is so profound that the hibernating animal cannot wake up quickly, even if it is disturbed. It takes at least 20 minutes to restore normal activity, and even then the animal is still quite cold and distinctly groggy, staggering about in a badly coordinated way.

Contrary to what many people believe, hibernating animals do not try to keep warm during the winter. They are better off being cold. This is because all chemical processes work faster at higher temperatures. Typically, at 10°C (50°F) warmer, the rate of chemical reactions is doubled. This includes the process by which fat is used to support the animal's metabolism – itself just a series of complex chemical reactions. So if a hibernating hedgehog were to be kept in a greenhouse or conservatory over winter, at a temperature of 15°C (59°F), it would burn up its fat reserves twice as fast as if it were kept at 5°C (41°F). Its reserves would then last only half as long, and it would probably die before the end of winter. In fact, the ideal temperature for a hibernating hedgehog is 4°C (39.2°F).

Stable refuge

The special place that a hibernating animal uses as a winter refuge is called a hibernaculum. It is important that the temperature inside should remain stable, because daily fluctuations in warmth disturb the animal's delicate physiology and cause more arousals, consuming vital fat reserves each time as the animal warms up. This is why a hedgehog builds a thick protective nest made of leaves in which to hibernate. The nest walls insulate the hedgehog and keep it close to its optimum hibernation temperature, regardless of the weather.

Bats also hibernate. They often seek out underground spaces such as caves, mines and cellars, which have cool, stable temperatures. Such sites are also humid, which is important – an inactive hibernator cannot get up to have a drink and risks becoming dehydrated. This is a particular problem for bats, because they lose a lot of water through evaporation from the thin, naked skin of their wings. Hibernating in a moist place reduces evaporation to a minimum.

A natterer's bat needs a cool place in which to hibernate. These bats often use caves, where they retreat into cracks in the walls. They may also wriggle into gaps in the brickwork of old tunnels. Such refuges help to protect them from predators.

◄ Like all the species of bat found in Britain, the whiskered bat feeds only on insects. Since these all but disappear in winter, the bat cannot find enough to eat, and hibernates in a cool, damp place, such as a cave or disused building. It usually hibernates alone, but sometimes in small groups of up to 20 individuals.

► A hibernating horseshoe bat wraps its wings around its body like a cloak. This increases the risk of moisture loss by evaporation, so these bats always select hibernation sites where the air is humid. Here their body temperatures fall so low that they often become covered in condensation droplets.

A hazel dormouse makes a tightly woven ball of shredded grass or other fibrous material, usually under dead leaves or moss, but sometimes beneath logs or among tree roots. Normally, hazel dormice and hedgehogs hibernate alone, but fat dormice often hibernate communally, with several animals – which are probably close relatives – passing the winter tightly curled up together. A fat dormouse makes no nest, but creeps down an existing hole such as an old rabbit, fox or badger burrow, a drain hole or a rotted-out tree root. Some slip beneath the floorboards of old houses or outbuildings, and simply lie on the bare earth. Insulated from the warmth of the winter sun, such sites normally remain at a constant low temperature.

People often assume that hibernation is a continuous state, with animals chilling down in about November and not waking up again until Easter. However, it seems that hibernators need to wake up every week or two. This may ensure that their systems keep working. Usually they do not leave their hibernation sites, but fall back into torpor after a few hours of drowsy consciousness.

It is normal for a hedgehog to wake up and change its nest at least once during winter, usually building a new one rather than re-occupying an existing nest. Bats frequently wake up during the winter and move to new quarters, usually in response to changes in the weather.

Winter home

Hedgehogs need plenty of dry leaves to build their winter nests, which is a good reason for not sweeping up all the fallen leaves in the garden.

Under cover of darkness, the hedgehog collects bundles of leaves in its mouth. Carrying a few at a time, it thrusts them into a heap beneath a hedge or pile of brushwood.

The hedgehog burrows inside and draws the leaves around itself to form a thick protective blanket.

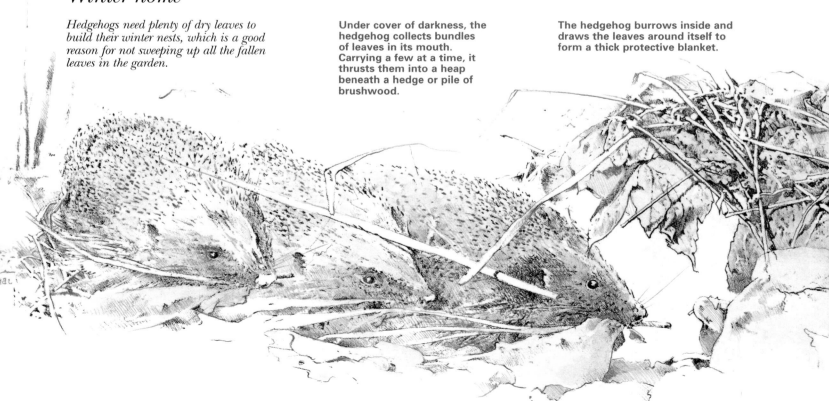

They seek out places with the best temperature conditions, choosing cooler places if the weather is warm, and sometimes warmer places during periods of intense cold.

Warming up

Arousal from hibernation is a more complex business than just waking up. The first stage is to raise the body temperature by burning up reserves of brown fat. This is a special type of fat stored around the shoulders under the skin. The purpose of this process is to generate enough heat to get the muscles working again. Once the animal can shiver and move about, the heat generated by its muscles is sufficient to restore its normal body temperature.

Its fat reserves also keep the animal alive during hibernation. Each time it arouses, it uses up a substantial part of its reserves, probably enough to last another ten days or more in hibernation. This is why it is vital that hibernators are not disturbed during the winter. They may have barely sufficient fat anyway, so if additional arousals caused by disturbance use up their supplies, they will not have enough to last the winter, and will die. Bats that hibernate in caves that are visited by people are particularly sensitive to this problem. This is why many major bat hibernation sites are now protected by gates to keep people out.

Winter sleep

Hedgehogs, dormice and bats are the only British mammals that adopt this winter strategy. It was once thought that badgers hibernated, but while they may remain underground during periods of

In hibernation, a hedgehog remains tightly rolled up for a few weeks at a time. This ensures that it cannot be attacked easily, even if a predator does manage to uncover it in its winter nest.

cold weather, they do not undergo the physiological changes experienced by true hibernators. Squirrels stay in their nests in bad weather, but their tracks may be seen in snow in the depths of winter. Even insects, amphibians and reptiles that lie dormant in winter are not true hibernators, because their temperatures are controlled by their environment all the time. They do not undergo the same radical transformation as warm-blooded mammals that go cold in winter.

WILDLIFE WATCH

How can I help hibernating animals?

● Hibernators are very sensitive to disturbance. Do not look for them, because each time they are disturbed they use up some of their precious fat reserves, which cannot be replaced by feeding. If you do find a hibernating animal in its nest, leave it alone.

● It is now illegal to disturb bats in their hibernation places. During the winter months, avoid entering any caves, cellars and old mines that are used by bats for hibernation. Even if you do not touch the bats, the sound of voices and the effect of body heat on the air temperature may combine to cause serious disturbance.

● Sometimes a hibernating hedgehog is found by accident in the garden, hidden under a pile of brushwood or leaves. It is best left alone or moved, with its nest, to another place. Bonfire heaps – including those built for Guy Fawkes' Night – should always be turned over before being lit, to rescue any hedgehogs that may be inside.

A fat dormouse hibernates underground, lying in close contact with the cool, damp soil. It makes no nest, but simply wraps its bushy tail around its body to help maintain a stable body temperature.

The robin

Fiercely territorial, the robin patrols its borders all year round. It declares ownership by singing loudly, sometimes even at night, and puffing out its brilliant orange-red breast feathers.

Many centuries ago robins would have been birds of the ancient woodland, favouring the forest edges and glades where a large tree had fallen. Over the years, these bold and adaptable birds have moved closer to human habitation and are now seen in city parks and suburban gardens as well as in woodlands, hedgerows and churchyards. They are found almost everywhere in the Britain Isles, except on the tops of high mountains and on islands remote from the mainland.

Robins are easily identified by their orange-red breasts and rotund shape. They are known for their tameness and will hop around while gardeners dig the beds, or perch boldly nearby, waiting for an earthworm or grub to be turned up. This daring behaviour gives robins an advantage over more timid species, enabling them to get to the food first.

Defending territories

The robin's image as a symbol of peace and goodwill at Christmas is rather misplaced because it is, in fact, one of the world's most aggressive birds. Most creatures sort out their disputes before one of them gets hurt, but not the robin. Fights to the death are not uncommon.

The worst fights are territorial disputes. Particular signals, understood by both parties, are employed by the territory holder as he patrols up and down the invisible frontier. At the first sign of a possible invasion he will fly up to a perch and puff out his red breast feathers to make them as prominent as possible.

If the encounter escalates, the robin may raise its head and tail, adopting a banana-like posture, and again confront the intruder with its puffed-up red breast. This display is usually enough to repel most rivals but if the intruder fails to retreat, battle may commence in earnest. The aggressive robin will try to attack its opponent's head, pecking at it violently. The eyes may be pecked out or the skull penetrated.

Unlike many other birds, robins defend their territory all year round. Winter quarters may not be the same as in summer, but borders are constantly patrolled. Females as well as males maintain their own winter territories, both sexes letting others know of their presence by singing.

◀ **When natural ponds may be frozen over, providing water for bathing and drinking is one way to attract a robin into the garden.**

▼ **A common sight in winter, the robin's distinctive colouring makes it unmistakable. It was officially adopted as Britain's national bird in 1960.**

ROBIN FACT FILE

The robin favours scrubby undergrowth for nesting, plus a few trees on which it can perch and proclaim its territory. Male and female robins have the same coloration, and when alarmed or frightened, they bob their heads and raise their tails.

● NAMES
Common name: robin, European robin
Scientific name: *Erithacus rubecula*

● HABITAT
Woodlands, copses and gardens, from remote, rural settings to the centre of cities

● DISTRIBUTION
Resident throughout British Isles except high mountains and Shetland; some seasonal movement

● STATUS
About 6.5 million pairs breed in the British Isles (about 2 million of them in Ireland)

● SIZE
Length 14cm (5½in); weight 16–22g (less than 1oz)

● KEY FEATURES
Adult has orange-red face and breast and whitish belly; juvenile has buff spots on upperparts and dark crescent markings below

● HABITS
Has separate winter and summer territories, which it defends aggressively; sings all year round, except in July, during the summer moult

● VOICE
Varied melodious, slightly melancholy song consisting of beautiful liquid warbling interspersed with harsher notes and sudden changes in tempo; high-pitched '*tseeee*' alarm call and aggressive '*tic tic*' call

● BREEDING
Late March to early July, sometimes as late as mid-August; 2, sometimes 3 broods

● FOOD
Insects and other invertebrates; small seeds and fruits, especially berries

● NEST
Built by the female; domed with a base of dead leaves lined with fine roots and mammal hair; in banks, tree stumps, walls (often among ivy), open-fronted nestboxes and various man-made sites

● EGGS
Usually 4–6 per clutch; white with red spots; incubation by female lasts 12–14 days

● YOUNG
Fed by both parents, they leave nest after 12–15 days, but remain dependent on their parents for up to 3 weeks

The brown plumage of a robin's upperparts, wings and tail provides good camouflage among the trees.

A bluish grey band separates the brown upperparts from the orange-red face and breast.

Distribution map key

■ Present all year round

□ Not present

Juvenile birds have speckled plumage and resemble young nightingales, although robins' tails are darker and shorter.

This young bird, undergoing its first moult, has almost acquired its full adult plumage, but the telltale speckly head reveals its youth.

Attacking an intruder

When a robin sees a rival in its territory, it quickly responds with a threat display. This follows a set sequence, progressively becoming more aggressive. If the intruder refuses to leave, the fight can end with bloodshed.

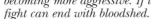

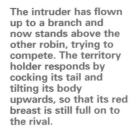
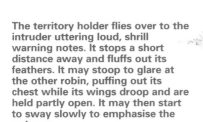

The territory holder flies over to the intruder uttering loud, shrill warning notes. It stops a short distance away and fluffs out its feathers. It may stoop to glare at the other robin, puffing out its chest while its wings droop and are held partly open. It may then start to sway slowly to emphasise the red area.

The intruder has flown up to a branch and now stands above the other robin, trying to compete. The territory holder responds by cocking its tail and tilting its body upwards, so that its red breast is still full on to the rival.

The challenge continues as the intruder flies at the territory holder. The two robins fall to the ground, the dominant bird raining pecks on the prone bird's head. An encounter such as this often ends in death.

Finding a mate

Generally, wild birds start to choose their mates in February, but robins may pair up early, from late December to early March. Courtship can get off to a slow start because the male robin does not always recognise a potential mate. He is often so concerned with defending his patch that he thinks an approaching female is an intruding male, and will try to drive her away. If the female persists by following the male around, he eventually accepts her and they combine territories, especially if, as often happens, the female's territory borders the male's. The new pair defend the extended area together, although during the breeding season the female leaves the territorial singing to her mate.

Usually, the female robin chooses the nest site and builds the nest. At this time courtship feeding begins – the female calls to her mate as a hungry nestling would do, and he responds by offering her a beakful of food. These extra supplies help build up the female's energy reserves. If all goes well, the pair will stay together through the breeding season, producing two or three clutches. The male takes over care of the first brood as the female prepares for the next. However, if the first breeding attempt fails, the pair are likely to split up and breed with different mates. Indeed, this sometimes happens even when the first brood has been reared successfully.

◄ **In readiness for a new brood of youngsters, a female robin busily collects leaves and other material to make her nest. In this task, she has no help from the male.**

This female (right) is being fed by her mate. This is part of the robin's mating ritual. It ensures that the female has enough nutrients to see her through the energy-demanding process of egg laying and incubation.

ROBIN CALENDAR

JANUARY ● FEBRUARY

Robins are 'early birds' – they may start pairing up as early as Christmas. A female notices the territorial male singing his loud spring song and approaches him. At first he tries to drive her off, but as she persists the male gradually accepts her.

MARCH ● APRIL

By the end of March, many robins will have mated and already have their first clutch of eggs. The female lays one egg a day but does not start incubation until the clutch is complete. Over this period she spends most of her time on the nest and the male brings her food.

MAY ● JUNE

Many nests are now full of hungry youngsters. Newly hatched robins are naked apart from tufts of dark fluffy down, and are totally dependent on their parents. By four days old they can stand up in the nest and beg for food, which is provided by both parents.

JULY ● AUGUST

About three weeks after leaving the nest young robins become independent, but they don't yet look like their parents. At this stage their plumage is speckled. Over the next two months they will gradually assume the typical red breast of the adult.

SEPTEMBER ● OCTOBER

In autumn, male and female robins go their separate ways, and each sets up a territory for the winter. Choice of territory is important because it must provide sufficient food for the owner to survive until spring. The robin defends its patch against interlopers by singing and vigorously displaying its red breast.

NOVEMBER ● DECEMBER

In severe weather, and especially in situations where food is abundant, the resident robin may allow others to come and feed on its patch. As a result, in winter a garden feeding table may offer the unusual and rewarding sight of several robins feeding together.

Where can I see robins?

● Robins are easy to observe since they are common throughout almost the whole of the British Isles. Parks and gardens in towns, cities and suburban areas, plus woodland, are favoured habitats.

● In winter, numbers may be swelled in eastern and southern Britain by immigrants from northern Europe. These are shyer than resident birds and have a paler, duller plumage.

● Robins' nests are notoriously difficult to find, tucked away in the hollow of a bank or behind a tangle of ivy. Often the first a householder knows of its presence is when an adult robin appears with a couple of speckled youngsters.

● Robins are well known for nesting in very odd places. The pockets of old gardening jackets hung behind the shed door are popular, along with old boots, shelves and piles of pots. Engines also seem to attract the birds. The prize for 'most remarkable robin nest' must surely go to one built precariously on the handle of a toilet flush.

● You can encourage robins into the garden by providing suitable food and by putting up nestboxes.

A male robin sometimes takes two mates, the second female building a nest in the first pair's territory. Few of these *ménages à trois* seem to be successful. The burden of trying to feed two females and two broods at about the same time is probably too much for all but the strongest of cock robins.

If one of a pair is lost during the breeding season – to a predator for instance – the survivor will try to pair up again within hours. The robin has just a few years of life and its top priority must be to pass on its genes to succeeding generations.

Causes of death

Whatever else a robin dies of, it almost certainly isn't old age. Of 5000 birds ringed and subsequently found dead, the oldest had lived for eight years and five months. However, the vast majority of those that hatch die as nestlings and recently fledged juveniles. Just over a quarter live for a year or more.

Domestic cats are one significant cause of death. Robins are also killed on the roads and some become accidentally trapped in buildings and starve to death. They may also be caught in traps set for other species – mice are actually not all that keen on cheese, but robins are.

Causes unconnected with man, such as natural predators, food shortages, attack by another robin and severe weather,

▲ Contrary to its appearance, this is not a particularly fat robin. In this case, the bird is simply protecting itself against the elements. Feathers are designed to trap air as insulation and, like other birds, robins fluff theirs up to keep warm in winter.

▼ Robins sing all year round. After the autumn moult the song sounds more wistful; it becomes stronger and more assertive in the new year.

result in the majority of fatalities. It is probable that most robins die unseen by human beings.

Enthusiastic singer

The robin is one of the earliest birds in the dawn chorus, and it is also one of the last to stop, often continuing well into twilight. In built-up areas robins can be heard singing at any time of the night, usually sparked off by street lamps or floodlights.

People who have heard a robin singing in the night often believe they have been listening to a nightingale, but time and place can rule this out. The nightingale, a summer visitor, is essentially restricted to the southern half of England, and its song can be heard spasmodically from mid-April to June. The robin is resident all year round and can be heard in any month except July. In fact, the nightingale that famously sang in London's Berkeley Square may indeed have been a robin.

This robin has nested in a garden shed. As long as there isn't too much disturbance and they can easily fly to and fro, robins will readily make use of man-made sites.

ENCOURAGING ROBINS

◄ **An open-fronted nestbox must be sited somewhere quiet, sheltered and not too near the ground, so the young are safe from predators.**

► **A dish of mealworms will undoubtedly attract a robin, although it's better to use a bird table or a birdfeeder than to place the dish on the ground. This leaves the birds vulnerable to their most deadly predator, the domestic cat.**

At any time of year, but especially in the winter, a bird table with birdseed and scraps, nut feeders and water for drinking and bathing will attract robins, as well as several other species, to the garden. Remember, though, that once birds come to expect and rely on finding food in the garden, it is important to put it out every day.

Many robins have learned to hang on peanut holders and help themselves, but although peanuts are good for tits and finches, they are not ideal for robins. They prefer a more 'meaty' diet – fat and cheese

are very popular, as are breadcrumbs and cake, plus a scattering of sultanas. Much of the food that robins like comes under the heading of 'household scraps'. One of the robin's favourite foods, however, is not likely to appear on any human dinner table – robins adore mealworms. These can be purchased without too much difficulty.

A good selection of shrubs and a few trees provide shelter and attractive places for a robin to perch and sing, which is important in establishing territory in both winter and summer. Robins are eclectic

and adaptable in their choice of nest sites, but will readily take to commercially available open-fronted nestboxes hung in the garden. Avoid the kind with a small round hole, which are suited to tits and other hole-nesters.

Site the box in an appropriate place. Robins avoid nesting in exposed sites, so it is best to conceal the box among ivy, honeysuckle or other climbing plants. Position it at about shoulder height but note that viewing a nesting bird once a day is too often – visits should be less frequent or the birds may become alarmed and abandon the nest.

To protect the nest from the attention of cats, enclose the box in a covering of

5cm (2in) mesh chicken wire. This will keep cats out but allow the robins to pass freely to and fro.

In winter, when the robins have moved on, remove the old nest before it decays and becomes infested with parasites. Leave the box ready for next year's birds.

The blue tit

Prominent among the different species of songbirds that visit the garden, especially when food is scarce, the blue tit can often be seen clinging to fence posts or birdfeeders.

Britain, along with Spain and Germany, probably has one of the largest blue tit populations in Europe. One recent estimate puts numbers at over three million pairs breeding in the British Isles each year, with some 20 million birds hatched. Although the survival rate is relatively low, the sheer numbers involved explain why this little bird can be sighted in these islands all year round.

Winter flocks are often mixed, sincluding the occasional nuthatch and treecreeper as well as great tits and coal tits. Ringing has shown that in winter many of these flocks stray no farther than a few hundred metres over woodland, parks and gardens. Some individuals may be more nomadic, but very few travel more than 10km (6 miles).

As woodland birds, blue tits scour tree tops, plucking insects from twigs and bark, but when food is scarce, they may visit reedbeds or low scrub. They are adaptable in their diet, eating seeds, fruit and household scraps as well as insects, and they are resourceful when it comes to finding food. In the days when bottled full-fat milk was delivered to every doorstep, blue tits were renowned for pecking through the foil tops to reach the fat-rich cream that had risen to the top. They still peck putty from window frames and strip moss from roofs.

FINE FEATHERS

On close inspection it becomes evident that plumage varies between different blue tits. Not only do the birds moult from their distinctive yellowish juvenile plumage in the autumn but their first winter feathers are different from the ones they display in their second winter. This is because the young birds keep their main wing and tail feathers until they are 15 months old. The primary coverts are also retained, as are some of the greater coverts. These appear greenish against the clearer blue of the new ones. This is easiest to see in males because their plumage is brighter than the more powdery blue of the females. The sexes also differ in size. Males are larger and the biggest males may be almost 20 per cent longer in the wing than the average female.

The yellow feathers of an adult blue tit have a dark base, often forming a grey line down the belly where the feathers part.

BLUE TIT FACT FILE

Blue tits evolved as a woodland species, and their short, thick, strong bills equip them well for collecting insects from crevices in the bark of trees. During the summer they spend most of their time feeding in the tops of trees, but will also forage on the ground in the winter.

● NAMES
Common name: blue tit
Scientific name: *Parus caeruleus*

● HABITAT
Wherever there are trees for nesting and feeding; mainly found in deciduous woodland but also in mixed and coniferous woods, parks, gardens and hedgerows; absent from mountain tops, open moorland and the seashore; may leave the highest, coldest woodland during winter, when they will visit scrubby areas and reedbeds to find food

● DISTRIBUTION
Common throughout the British Isles

● STATUS
3.3 million breeding pairs in British Isles

● SIZE
Length 11.5cm (4½in); weight 10–12g (½oz)

● KEY FEATURES
Generally blue with green, white and yellow markings; blue crown; much smaller than great tit; stubby, conical bill; thick, short neck; juveniles much yellower than adults

● HABITS
Very agile; often hangs upside down to feed; sociable outside breeding season

● VOICE
Song rather variable within limits, usually two or three high-pitched, thin and clear *'tsee-tsee-tsee'* notes or *'tsee-tsee-tsee-tsit'*, followed by a rapid liquid churring trill; various other churring and scolding calls

● FOOD
Insects and spiders, seeds, fruit, buds; peanuts, sunflower seeds and fat from garden feeders; caterpillars are important for young

● BREEDING
Usually starts in late April/early May, timed so that the arrival of hungry chicks in the nest coincides with the flush of caterpillars in deciduous forest trees; second broods rarely recorded in Britain

● NEST
Always in a hole or crevice, whether in a tree, wall, building or even a bus-stop sign; nestboxes readily adopted; nest is a cosy cup of moss, grass and plant fibres, lined with soft feathers and hair or wool

● EGGS
Rounded and white with sparse, dull red markings; clutch 7–13 or more (sometimes up to 16) in natural habitats, but smaller in gardens; incubated for two weeks or so from when last egg is laid

● YOUNG
Remain in nest for 16–22 days

Blue tits are pugnacious birds and will often tackle surprisingly large prey, such as this moth.

A blue cap tops the mainly white face.

Back feathers are greenish blue.

A single narrow white bar adorns the bright blue wings.

The intensity of colour of the yellowish underparts varies between individuals. Males tend to be brighter.

As with all birds, bathing is an important ritual for blue tits. It helps to keep their feathers clean and free of parasites.

Distribution map key

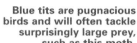

Present all year round

Not present

◀ A tree hole is a natural nest site for a blue tit, providing eggs and young with some degree of protection from predators.

Cooperative behaviour

Living in flocks in winter and operating collectively is essential for the survival of these small birds. One benefit is that all the birds are constantly on the look-out for a cat, sparrowhawk or other predator in the vicinity, and can make good their escape at the first hint of trouble. A few rapid calls, the scolding 'churr-rr-rr' of alarm, will scatter them to a variety of safe perches.

In the constant search for food, the chances of success are increased if the birds comb an area together. Some will fly ahead while others, having come across a possible source of food, stay behind to investigate a particular bush or tree. Those in the advance guard soon realise they are missing a meal and quickly return. Likewise, among reedbeds in winter, the birds alert each other to any food they may find.

▲ A newly fledged blue tit lacks the intensity of colour seen in the plumage of adult birds, but the facial patterning is essentially the same.

BLUE TIT CALENDAR

JANUARY ● FEBRUARY

The days are getting longer but food supplies are still depleted and the birds come under pressure during prolonged cold spells. Most tits are still living in large, mixed flocks, but are beginning to investigate breeding territories.

MARCH ● APRIL

Singing and territorial activity increases, and by mid-April each pair will have chosen the year's nest site and be nest building. The earliest eggs – rounded and white with dull red markings – are laid at the end of April.

MAY ● JUNE

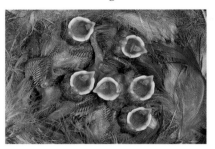

The young hatch and a nestful may demand up to 1000 feeds a day. By the end of June, the youngsters have left the nest and formed small flocks of their own, but they are not yet independent of the adults.

JULY ● AUGUST

The flocks of fledglings now roam around without the adults and attract other families of tits as well as warblers, treecreepers, nuthatches, goldcrests and other species. The adults undergo their full moult.

SEPTEMBER ● OCTOBER

The juvenile flocks are rejoined by the adults but the birds soon begin to disperse. Some adults will move a few kilometres to winter areas they have used before, while some youngsters will relocate up to 10km (6 miles) away.

NOVEMBER ● DECEMBER

Overwintering areas are occupied by established flocks of tits. More time is spent in gardens as the autumn food stores become depleted. Providing birds with suitable high-energy food is of vital importance during the winter.

Acrobatic feeders

Blue tits are active and inquisitive birds. This curiosity stands them in good stead as they bustle about, foraging on bark and among catkins for caterpillars and other tiny or camouflaged insects.

A blue tit is so light it is able to perch on the thinnest twigs to obtain food.

Before eating, the bird scans the area to ensure it is safe. In the countryside, blue tits are prey to sparrowhawks, and in the garden, cats are a constant danger.

▲ **The colourful and beautifully patterned plumage of the blue tit is a common sight in suburban gardens. Males and females look alike.**

When it is reassured and any alarm calls have subsided, the blue tit begins to pick seeds from the catkin.

▲ **A blue tit may take just a few minutes to discover a new peanut feeder. Peanuts form quite a large part of the garden birds' diet and they are not alarmed by wire feeders.**

Garden visitors

Food and water in the garden are magnets for birds all year round and it can be difficult to assess exactly how many individuals are visiting. In one study, bird ringers identified more than 300 individual blue tits visiting one garden in one day. As a rough guide, if five blue tits come to a feeder at the same time, the chances are that 50 different birds are visiting each day, and 500 individuals may come over the course of a year. Numbers fluctuate, of course, mainly due to the severity of winter and the availability of food during the breeding season.

Short lives

The huge numbers of blue tits hatched each year are just enough to replace the birds lost, which is essential to maintain a healthy population. It is estimated that around 15 million blue tits die each year in Britain, some from disease or starvation but many are eaten by sparrowhawks. These stealthy, agile predators specialise in snatching small birds from cover, although they will also capture them in mid-flight.

Blue tit fledglings are particularly vulnerable, as are any birds that are weak or injured. When sparrowhawks have nestlings themselves, in late June and July, they may eat up to a third of the newly fledged blue tits. This predation has no effect on the breeding population of blue tits the following year. In fact, it is an

▼**A blue tit will use all manner of man-made objects for nesting. Any structure that gives protection from the elements and from predators will do.**

effective way of ensuring that only the fittest and healthiest survive to pass on their genes.

Domestic cats account for a fair proportion of blue tit deaths. Large numbers of birds perish in collisions with house windows, dying either as a direct result of the impact, or when opportunistic cats take advantage of the stunned birds.

Nest sites

Blue tits form long-term relationships within the flock and bird ringers often recatch the same birds together after a period of many months. The boldest ones are most likely to be adult males.

Both male and female search for a place to build their nest in the spring, investigating holes in trees, buildings and man-made nestboxes, but the female makes the final choice. When a male finds a suitable place, he bobs up and down, fluttering his feathers and calling to his mate. Eventually, he hops inside the hole and the female may follow him. She inspects each site, rejecting several before deciding upon one she likes. She then sets about building a nest, collecting grass, moss and small twigs before lining it with any soft material she can find, such as fur, wool and even human hair. After the last egg is laid, the female settles down for the next two weeks or so to incubate the clutch.

If the pair have nested in a garden, they may face a problem once the young have hatched. Although the nest site is chosen carefully, many birds find themselves too far away from any big native trees to be able to find the rich supply of caterpillars they rely upon to feed their young. Large oaks and beeches are not normally found in suburban gardens and even small native trees – hawthorn, alder, rowan or birch – are often in short supply. The trees most commonly found in gardens are small and exotic, from China or America. They tend not to support native insects and so are not productive hunting grounds for blue tits, especially in the summer months. The adult birds have a frantic time trying to find enough live food to sustain their offspring.

A big brood takes up to 1000 feeds a day in the forest and the chicks generally all survive. In the garden, fewer eggs are laid and the broods are often depleted by lack of food. Many people stop putting food out for the birds in summer, assuming that it is not needed, but the adults are expending great amounts of energy at this time. Birdfeeders stocked with nuts and seeds feed the adults so that they can use all the insects they find for their young. Mealworms placed on a bird table will be readily accepted by the adults to take into the nest, but do not put out fly maggots as these are too big for the chicks.

Winter roosts

Sometimes the nest site doubles as a winter roost but all sorts of other holes, nooks and crannies may be used, too.

▼ Its long, hooked claws allow the blue tit to cling to brickwork. The bird spends some moments checking that the coast is clear before entering its nearby nest to feed its young.

▲ In the first few days after hatching, blue tit chicks are essentially naked and defenceless. The female incubates them for up to 16 days, until a covering of feathers provides them with some insulation.

DETERRING PREDATORS

Strategically positioned bamboo canes will help disrupt the hunting flights of sparrowhawks, the main predator of the blue tit. Push the canes into the ground around birdfeeders, where they will deter the birds of prey but the tits will ignore them.

To prevent window collisions, stick cut-out silhouettes of hawks or other birds to the windows. Ready-made cut-outs are available from the RSPB.

Make sure all feeders, bird tables, suspended coconut halves and nestboxes are out of reach of cats. Do not leave food for the birds on the ground, especially in the winter when tits are more likely to be encouraged to search on the ground and among low-level vegetation.

BLUE TIT NESTBOXES

Most gardens need three nestboxes – one each for blue tits and great tits and a spare. Ready-made versions come in all shapes and sizes and are available from the RSPB and garden centres. However, no particular skill is needed to make a blue tit nestbox at home, although a few points should be borne in mind:

● Use reasonably thick wood to provide good insulation when the weather is either hot or cold. The birds use the box for roosting in the winter and may decide not to use it for breeding if it is cold or draughty.

● The floor area should be about 14cm (5½in) square. Smaller than that would be cramped and may restrict the number of eggs laid.

● The entrance hole should be no bigger than 25mm (1in) across, to keep out great tits, house sparrows and predators.

● Do not put a perch by the entrance hole because this would be an invitation for predators.

● The chicks may generate a lot of moisture. Condensation will make the box damp and unhealthy unless it has reasonable ventilation.

● The box should not face south because it may become too hot in summer.

● Site the box in a place that is sheltered from wind and rain, and not too close to feeders. The proximity of other birds would disturb the nest.

● A hinged top on the box means that an eye can be kept on what is happening inside, but be careful not to disturb an incubating bird. A hinged lid also makes cleaning the box at the end of the breeding season easier. All nest debris should be removed to avoid the build-up of parasites. When doing this, wear protective gloves because some bird parasites will bite humans, causing skin irritation. Do not use pesticides because these will be harmful for the birds.

● As an alternative to making a nestbox, invest in a woodcrete palace. These unusually named constructions are made out of sawdust and concrete and are guaranteed for 25 years. They are distributed by Jacobi Jayne and Company, telephone 01227 714311 or visit www.jacobijayne.co.uk. Woodcrete boxes have been shown to give blue tits a greater chance of breeding success than ordinary nestboxes, and the birds often prefer them.

▲ In the garden, a nestbox is often chosen in preference to shrubs and small trees as a nest site and also as a winter roost.

▲ At the first sight or sound of a parent returning to the nest with food, the young blue tits start calling and begging to be fed. The most active, and therefore healthiest, chick will be fed first. In this way, the fittest chicks survive.

The roosts are often difficult to locate because the birds enter them at dusk, just as the light is fading, possibly to escape the notice of predators. One tell-tale sign is a little heap of droppings that may build up on the ground below.

A most unusual, yet highly practical roosting site was discovered in the lamp-holders of 1960s street lamps. The lamps had a convenient hole leading into a small space above the bulb but shielded from it by the reflector. Where these lamps were installed, tits often took advantage of the warm and cosy space.

WILDLIFE WATCH

Where can I see blue tits?

● Woodland, gardens, parks – blue tits are found wherever there are trees. They are very easy to see and are usually quite noisy as the birds in the flock call to each other.

▶ Inside the nestbox, the sight of gaping pinkish mouths is the signal that encourages the parent bird to release its supply of caterpillars and other insect grubs.

Distorted beaks

Blue tits seldom have distinguishing plumage traits, such as the flecks of white that enable birdwatchers to tell blackbirds apart in some areas. However, many records exist of blue tits with amazingly distorted beaks.

The material of the bill grows continuously and should the tip be damaged – so that the upper and lower parts of the beak (known as mandibles) do not wear against each other – the bills develop into sickle shapes or become crossed like scissors. This clearly makes feeding very difficult and it is surprising that a bird affected in this way is able to survive at all. It will look very scruffy because it is unable to preen its feathers efficiently. Eventually, the overgrown bill snaps off, allowing the tips to meet and the beak to return to its normal shape.

The dunnock

Although it is generally solitary, except during the mating season, this very common but inconspicuous brown bird often draws attention to itself with its unusual way of moving, combining odd, low, jerky hops and a fast-flicking tail.

An unobtrusive little bird, the dunnock is often mistaken for other species and sometimes, strangely, for a mouse. Indeed, the Dutch name for the dunnock is *heggemus*, meaning 'hedge mouse'. Even without misidentification, the dunnock has had many names. In medieval times, according to the poet Geoffrey Chaucer, it was *heysugge*, meaning 'hedge flutterer'. Later the bird became known as the hedge sparrow, because it looks quite like a sparrow and nests in hedges. Today the name dunnock – descriptive of its dun colour – is preferred because, although it shares certain traits with sparrows, it is not actually a member of the same family.

It belongs to a small family of 13 species called the accentors (pronounced 'acksentors'), or Prunellidae, most of which breed in the mountainous regions of Central Asia. The dunnock is the only member of this group regularly found in

Britain. The British Ornithological Union has recently proposed giving the bird yet another name – the hedge accentor.

Recognisable song

One of the best ways to identify the dunnock is by its song. This is delivered in short warbling bursts and has been likened to a snatch of ragtime piano music. Walk beside a hedgerow after an April shower, while the air is fresh and still, and the first bird to start singing is most likely to be a dunnock.

Its scurrying, shuffling gait is another distinctive feature. The bird moves with a series of very short, low hops, one foot held just in front of the other, with legs slightly bent. Frequent and extremely fast flicks of its wings and tail accompany many of its movements.

The dunnock's beak is narrow and pointed – a typical insect-eater's bill – and differs completely from the sturdy,

conical beaks of most seed-eaters. Although the dunnock is primarily insectivorous, it will also eat seeds when insects are in short supply. This makes dunnocks easy to watch in winter. Simply scatter some seed on the ground and wait for hungry birds to find them. Dunnocks are not tame but seem undisturbed by the near presence of humans. Using foreign finch seed, which is much smaller than the seed found in most conventional wild bird food mixtures, means the dunnocks will take more time to pick them up, giving anyone watching a good opportunity to see the birds properly. They will also search the ground under peanut feeders for the tiniest morsels dropped by untidy tits and finches.

The dunnock creeps among dense vegetation or beneath hedges, hunting for insects by flicking over small leaves and probing the debris with its beak.

DUNNOCK FACT FILE

A plump but sleek little songbird, the dunnock is common in gardens and parks and may even use the handle of a gardener's fork as a songpost. Individuals or pairs are often seen hopping and shuffling in the herbaceous border as they forage for tiny insects.

● NAMES
Common names: dunnock, hedge sparrow, hedge accentor
Scientific name: *Prunella modularis*

● HABITAT
Gardens, parks, copses, hedgerows, open woodland, heaths, scrubland and young conifer plantations

● DISTRIBUTION
Widespread and abundant throughout British Isles; absent from a few Scottish islands

● STATUS
Estimated at about 2,000,000 territories in Britain and 700,000–850,000 in Ireland; the cause of a rapid decline in total population between 1970 and the 1980s is not known

● SIZE
Length 14.5cm (5¾in); weight 18–21g (about ¾oz); males have very slightly longer wings

● KEY FEATURES
Plumage is warm brown, broadly streaked, darker on its back; neck, throat and breast soft grey tinged with slate blue – brightest in breeding season and males usually brighter than females; ear coverts and crown are browner, with dark markings; narrow buff wingbar; juveniles more spotted and streaky than adults

● HABITS
Creeping mouse-like gait; light, jerky flight; sings throughout year; solitary except in autumn; sedentary

● VOICE
Insistent, somewhat plaintive, shrill *'dzeep'*, usually uttered from cover as warning or contact call; song a short, fast, high-pitched warbling phrase

● FOOD
Beetles, snails, spiders, flies, earthworms and springtails; seeds and berries in autumn and winter

● BREEDING
2–3 broods raised from April–late August

● NEST
A fairly substantial cup of twigs, leaves, rootlets and grass, lined with moss, wool, hair and feathers; sited in bush, hedge or low tree 15–150cm (6in–5ft) above ground

● EGGS
4–6 (rarely 3 or 7) deep blue, unmarked, rather pointed; incubated for 10–13 days by female

● YOUNG
Fed by parents; fledge at 11–12 days

A young dunnock has a dull brown iris but this changes to a brighter, more reddish colour when it matures. The bill is fine, tapering to a point and is used mainly to glean insects from leaf litter.

Distribution map key

■	Present all year round
□	Not present

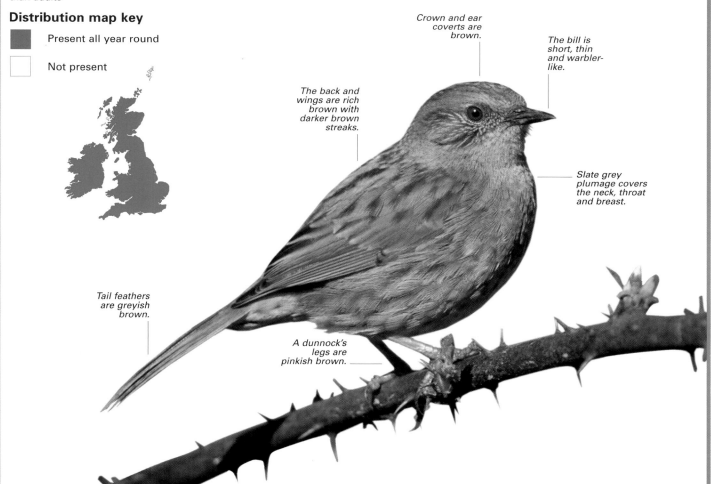

Crown and ear coverts are brown.

The bill is short, thin and warbler-like.

The back and wings are rich brown with darker brown streaks.

Slate grey plumage covers the neck, throat and breast.

Tail feathers are greyish brown.

A dunnock's legs are pinkish brown.

Other birds will, of course, flock to the birdseed, too, including house sparrows, but with a little experience, it becomes easy to pick out the dunnocks. Slimmer and less bulky than the sparrow, the dunnock's plumage is at first similar, essentially brown and streaky. However, this colouring changes with age, and significant differences are apparent between the adult plumage of dunnocks and sparrows. Mature dunnocks have a warm bluish grey neck and breast, in contrast to the duller greyish or buff underparts of the sparrow.

Many partners

The dunnock is extremely active during the breeding season. Although some are monogamous, many are polygamous, and this behaviour results in all kinds of complicated matings. One female may pair with two males, or two females with one male, or two or three males with two to four females. A male is always on the look out for amorous engagements and the fact that he may already have a mate makes no difference. If he is fortunate, he will mate with up to four females during the four or five months of the breeding season.

The male dunnock is well equipped for his sexual marathon. In those bird species in which the male and female are more or less indistinguishable on the basis of their plumage, ornithologists use breeding features to separate them – namely the brood patch in females and the genital profile in males. The males of most bird species do not have penises. Instead, they have what is known as a cloacal protruberance, which swells when they are sexually active. This is a modest size in most birds – robins and wrens for example – but it is large and unmistakable in the dunnock. Prominent and full of sperm, it improves the chances of every encounter resulting in young.

For their part, female dunnocks are just as enthusiastic about mating as the males. A female may have a mate – she may even be sitting on her nest with a clutch of eggs beneath her – but she is only too happy to attract the attention of any passing male.

Female allure

Dunnocks are unusual among small birds because both males and females often seek out multiple partners to mate with. Males roam around searching for willing consorts and females actively seduce as many partners as possible. Their pre-copulation display is an elaborate dance.

A male notices a female visitor. Courtship involves a distinctive 'wing-waving' display in which he flicks open his wings and waves them over his back while uttering a shrill call.

The female solicits the male's attention by 'wing-shivering'. She shows she is ready to copulate by raising her tail and running round in small circles.

The male gives chase, but if his attention lapses for one moment, the female may slip away to mate with another nearby male before returning.

The female crouches, ruffling her body feathers and shivering her wings. She quivers her tail, raising it high to expose her cloaca to the male.

DUNNOCK CALENDAR

JANUARY • FEBRUARY

Winter is a lean time for dunnocks. They are most likely to be seen at garden feeders early in the year, gleaning what they can from the ground. Bad weather also leads to a peak mortality rate.

MARCH • APRIL

Nest building begins from late March and continues throughout April. Territorial song and disputes increase in intensity. The females, with their mates in attendance, gather nesting materials.

MAY • JUNE

Most first-brood young will have hatched by May. This is a busy time for the adults as they feed their ever-hungry young. Fortunately the warmer temperatures provide an abundance of insect prey.

JULY • AUGUST

In early July, the last clutches of the year are laid. By late August, the young from this year's first broods will have fledged. Some adults have completed their moult by late August.

SEPTEMBER • OCTOBER

Dunnocks are usually solitary, but may form loose flocks at this time. The birds exhibit 'migratory restlessness' at coastal sites, but rarely move more than a kilometre from their breeding territory.

NOVEMBER • DECEMBER

As the days get shorter and the temperature drops, dunnocks spend all their time searching for food. Preening keeps the plumage in peak condition for cold and wet spells.

Bearing in mind that all animal behaviour, however surprising it may seem, has a survival value, it is not difficult to account for the dunnock's conduct. Quite simply, every mating increases the chances of females laying fertile eggs. Each male tries to ensure his genes are passed on. He will hop from side to side behind the female, pecking at her cloaca for up to two minutes in an attempt to make her eject any sperm from a recent mating. However, DNA testing has revealed that the youngsters in any brood, while sharing the same mother, often have more than one father. Therefore, not only is the probability of fertility increased, but there is a healthy mixing of the gene pool – another essential element in the stability and survival of the species.

Careful builders

Dunnocks are excellent homemakers and exemplary parents. They select and defend territories, often as a female with two males, and begin the business of building a nest in early spring.

The nest, which is constructed solely by the female, is usually well hidden in a hedge or bush. Sturdily built on a foundation of twigs, and up to 15cm (6in) across, the main structure is made of moss woven with leaves, rootlets and grass. This is lined with wool, hair and feathers, making it cosy and warm, and a perfect setting for the dunnock's beautifully coloured eggs. These are deep pure blue with a gloss – almost a turquoise glow – that seems to reflect the blue of the sky when seen in the half-light of a hedge or bush.

Having created a safe home and laid a clutch of usually four to six eggs, the female incubates them for about 12 days. In a further 12 days or so after hatching, the young fledge. Then the female will

Copulation is exceptionally brief. The male appears to jump over the female, the genital contact lasting only a fraction of a second.

The dunnock's song is a lively and cheerful brief warble. It can be heard at any time of the year, but especially in the breeding season, when it is uttered from the top of a bush or other songpost.

start a second and later perhaps even a third family, sometimes nurturing up to 18 chicks per breeding season. This might seem to be a prodigious output, but many chicks are lost to predators, bad weather or parasitism – in the form of a cuckoo in the nest.

Close to home

British dunnocks rarely move far away from their home territories – almost all retrapped ringed birds are caught within 10km (6 miles) of where they were first caught.

Continental dunnocks and other accentor species do make cold weather migrations and an occasional dunnock from the Low Countries or even Scandinavia is recorded in Britain, usually at coastal ringing sites.

Interestingly, movements of flocks of dunnocks are sometimes noted at coastal observatories in autumn, but there is no evidence to suggest that they ever actually leave British shores. One explanation for this odd behaviour is that it is a hangover from the time when dunnocks inhabited mountainous forests, and migrated down to milder areas in winter. In Scotland, they still breed at altitudes of 500m (1640ft) or more in juniper scrub. However, today's residents have largely forsaken their original surroundings for a new habitat. About 200 years ago, they moved from mountain conifer forests into gardens, hedgerows and small woodlands. So while they no longer need to move to warmer climes in winter, they may, perhaps, still retain an ancestral migration instinct.

A CUCKOO IN THE NEST

The dunnock is a favourite host of the cuckoo, especially in central and southern England – hence its nicknames of 'blind dunnock' or 'fool sparrow'. Other common hosts include the reed warbler (in reedbeds), the meadow pipit (on moorland), the robin (in similar habitats to dunnocks) and the pied wagtail (in open country). Over 50 different host species have been recorded in Britain for the cuckoo, but these are the five main ones, accounting for 90 per cent of all instances.

In spring, cuckoos can be seen searching hedgerows and other suitable nesting areas for dunnock nests. The female spends many hours watching the host nest to ensure that she deposits her egg at exactly the right time – that is, when the dunnock is laying her eggs and before she has started to incubate them.

The cuckoo's strategy is to remove one of the dunnock's eggs and replace it with one of her own. In most cases she will match the colour of her own egg to those already in the nest, so it is possible that the parent birds do not recognise the impostor, despite it usually being a larger size. However, the female cuckoo does not bother to replicate the turquoise of the dunnock's eggs, so the replacement should be obvious. Strangely though, the dunnock appears to notice nothing untoward and is an obliging foster parent. Fortunately, such parasitism has no effect on the size and health of the overall population of the dunnock.

A baby cuckoo dwarfs its devoted foster parent. It will have pushed most of the dunnock's own eggs or offspring out of the nest as soon as it hatched. With one female and perhaps two males providing food, the youngster grows fast.

WILDLIFE WATCH

Where can I see dunnocks?

● Dunnocks will be present in almost any garden that provides cover and food. Watch out for them in shrub borders and on the ground beneath birdfeeders. Also, always check a ground-feeding flock of house sparrows for the occasional dunnock mingling quietly among them.

● Dunnocks tend to stay behind after other species have left, searching the ground for the tiniest fragments that have fallen from the birdfeeders or bird table.

● Listen for the dunnock's short, penetrating, shrill, piping 'dzeep' call or a burst of song as you walk beside any hedgerow. The call is often given from cover, but as the bird usually sits near or on the top of the hedge to deliver its song, it is quite easy to spot.

● Dunnocks are present in woodland too, but here they are more often skulking, and are only likely to be seen at the edges of clearings or paths.

As winter approaches and the temperature drops, it becomes more important than ever for the dunnock to keep its plumage in good condition. Regular preening and bathing at the margins of ponds or lakes keep the feathers in peak condition to provide maximum insulation against the onslaught of cold and wet weather.

The devil's coach horse

An aggressively raised tail makes this beetle look rather like a scorpion, but instead of a sting, it is equipped with glands that exude a pungent secretion – a potent defence against predators.

One of the favourite haunts of the devil's coach horse is the compost heap, especially in winter when it benefits from the extra warmth generated by rotting debris. A garden beetle, it tends to hide under any convenient cover during the day. It may creep under flowerpots, especially in greenhouses, where it is also warmer in winter and it may even take up residence in older, damper buildings. Sometimes campers are alarmed by the noise of these beetles struggling to escape from beneath a tent's groundsheet.

The devil's coach horse is a rove beetle, a member of the family Staphylinidae – often shortened to 'staphs' by entomologists. This is Britain's largest family of beetles, with almost 1000 native members. Rove beetles, many of which are just a few millimetres long, have very short wingcases, called elytra. These tough, modified forewings leave most of the abdomen exposed. Although the devil's coach horse appears to be wingless, its wings are neatly folded away under these tiny covers.

At 20–30mm (approximately 1in) long, the devil's coach horse is the biggest rove beetle in the British Isles. Because its heavy body is not ideal for flight, it keeps mainly to the ground, although it is in fact quite capable of flying.

A coating of fine hairs gives the beetle a matt black appearance, sometimes with a rusty red tinge. It is sometimes mistaken for a giant earwig, but the coach horse has no sign of the tail pincers that characterise that group of insects.

Defence mechanisms

When alarmed, the devil's coach horse opens its massive jaws, curves its abdomen forward over its thorax and exudes a

Faced with a threatening display, coupled with the release of a nauseating secretion, it takes a creature with a hearty appetite to take on a devil's coach horse.

pungent secretion from white glands at the tip. In this position, which has given the insect its alternative name of cock-tail beetle, it looks quite fierce.

If disturbed further, the devil's coach horse can fire nauseous streams of partly digested food from both ends. It can also deliver a fairly painful bite if it is handled roughly or feels threatened by an unwary shrew or other small mammal, but otherwise it is harmless.

DID YOU KNOW?

The derivation of the name 'devil's coach horse' is uncertain, but it possibly stems from medieval legend associating the beetle's colour and sinister defensive display with the devil. According to Irish mythology, the devil's curse – or even death – awaits anyone coming face to face with a displaying beetle.

Feeding and breeding

Few invertebrates are safe from the coach horse's formidable jaws. At night, the beetle wanders in search of prey and can be seen on garden paths and lawns. It feeds on slugs, worms, millipedes, woodlice, spiders, caterpillars and other insect grubs. It is also a scavenger, often found feeding on animal corpses or other decaying matter. Although it eats some insects that gardeners regard as useful, the coach horse is, on balance, to be welcomed in the garden.

Devil's coach horses normally mate towards the end of the summer, often under logs or stones, and the female lays her pearly white eggs in the soil. These are surprisingly large at 3mm (⅛in) long, and hatch within a few weeks. The larvae resemble the adults in shape and have the same powerful jaws and predatory habits, but the abdomen is dirty white and rather soft, and there are no wings. They pupate in the soil when fully grown and new adults emerge during the following summer. The adult beetles may live for several years – if they are not eaten first.

Numerous predators

Despite their alarming appearance and noxious secretions, devil's coach horses are eaten by many other animals.

Chickens and pheasants snap them up at every opportunity, as do blackbirds. Even the much smaller robin is not afraid to pursue these meaty morsels of food. Shrews and hedgehogs also eat them regularly, as do badgers and foxes.

Other enemies are more insidious. Tiny parasitic wasps lay their eggs in or on the beetle larvae. The wasp grubs feed on the living larvae and then pupate, clinging to the shrivelled corpses like clusters of minute white jelly-babies.

Philonthus fuscipennis, another rove beetle, looks almost identical to the devil's coach horse, but is shorter and stouter.

Close relations

Several rove beetles are superficially similar to the devil's coach horse, but a careful, close look may help to distinguish one from another. For example, *Philonthus politus* is slightly more rotund than the devil's coach horse and has even more formidable jaws. It can be recognised by its bronzy elytra. *Creophilus maxillosus* is a little smaller than the devil's coach horse, and has a lot of grey downy hair on its front wing cases, or elytra, and abdomen.

Velleius dilatatus, up to 24mm (1in) long, has a glossier head and thorax, and its antennae are strongly toothed. A rarely seen beetle, it lives in hornet nests and feeds on tree sap.

Some burying beetles – those that bury carcasses as food for their offspring – also resemble rove beetles, but their elytra are longer and only a few abdominal segments are exposed at the rear.

▲ A speedy runner by insect standards, this beetle can chase and capture even fast-moving invertebrate prey.

◄ The devil's coach horse has ferocious-looking jaws, which are strong enough to cut through the hard carapaces of other beetles. However, these outsize mandibles are too cumbersome to eat with, so the beetle uses an additional set of much smaller mouthparts, called maxillae, for manipulating pieces of food.

WILDLIFE WATCH

Where can I see devil's coach horse beetles?

● Common throughout the British Isles, these beetles are not likely to be seen during the day unless disturbed from their resting place among rubbish or under stones.

● They usually hide away during the coldest months, and the compost heap is a good place to find them in winter.

● Adult beetles can be found throughout the year, but they are most active from April to September.

● Go out into the garden at night and look for the beetles feeding on small insects and decaying animal matter.

Lacewings

Most of these delicate insects spend the winter as larvae, wrapped in silken cocoons, but one, the common green lacewing, seeks shelter in the warmth of human habitation.

The lacy networks of veins that support their wings give these fragile-looking insects their name. They are also known as lacewing flies, but this is misleading because they are not true flies of the order Diptera. They belong to a quite different order of insects, the Neuroptera.

Green lacewings and the smaller brown lacewings belong to two separate families. Altogether there are more than 60 species in Britain, from tiny insects with wings that span less than 12mm (½in), to the giant lacewing, which has a wingspan of about 50mm (2in). Despite their fragile appearance, most are voracious predators of aphids and other small insects.

Lacewings are mainly nocturnal, and several species are attracted to lighted windows at night. During the day they often roost among foliage with their wings held tent-like above their bodies. If they are disturbed, some will take to the air while others drop into the undergrowth.

Bright eyes

The green lacewings are the most familiar native species. Confusingly, two of these are actually brown, but they are rare. The

▶ **Despite their large wings, lacewings are weak and rather clumsy in flight. They rarely fly during the day unless disturbed from their resting places among vegetation.**

◀ **The huge eyes of the common green lacewing glow an iridescent gold when caught by the light.**

others are varying shades of green, often with a strong bluish cast. They can be recognised by the conspicuously forked veins at the outer edges of each wing. They also have bright, brassy compound eyes, and biting jaws for chewing their aphid prey.

Green lacewings attach their eggs to plants by slender stalks of quick-setting gum. These stalks may be separate, each bearing a single egg, or they may coalesce

into a thicker form and support several eggs. The bristly, shuttle-shaped larvae that hatch from the eggs are even more voracious than the adults. They prey on aphids too, but feed in a very different way. Each larva's long, curved jaws generally project well beyond its head and, although the jaws look substantial, they are actually hollow. Instead of using them to cut up aphids, the larva plunges them into its prey and uses them like drinking straws to drain the aphid's juices, leaving little more than an empty skin.

Since the larvae feed entirely on fluids, they produce no droppings. In fact, there is no connection between the front and rear parts of the gut.

▲ The lacewing larva preys on soft-bodied insects such as aphids. It pierces each aphid with its curved, hollow jaws and sucks out its body fluids.

▶ A green lacewing larva conceals itself from predatory birds under dried-out aphid skins and any other fragments of litter it can attach to its back.

The small amount of solid residue that does accumulate is not excreted until the larva turns into an adult.

When a lacewing larva has drained an aphid, it may discard the skin, but some larvae put the empty husks to good use. The larva flicks the corpse over onto its own back, where it sticks to the bristly, hooked hairs and provides excellent camouflage. Only the curved jaws protruding from the front end indicate that there is a living insect concealed under the pile of debris.

Winter routine

When they are mature, lacewing larvae spin silken cocoons in which to pupate. The silk is produced by modified excretory glands in the abdomen, not by the salivary glands as in most other insects. The majority of lacewings produce two or three generations each year. The final generation generally passes the winter in the form of a shrunken larva known as a pre-pupa, which remains in its cocoon and turns into a pupa in the spring. In one species,

however, adults hibernate for the winter. The common green lacewing *Chrysoperla carnea* may be found sleeping in houses and sheds. It loses its bright green colour in the autumn, becoming straw-coloured or pinkish until the spring.

Brown lacewings

The brown lacewings found in Britain belong to three different families that have different forms of wing veins. Individual species can be hard to identify. Two exceptions are the scarce *Drepanepteryx phalaenoides*, which can be recognised by its hooked wingtips, and the giant lacewing *Osmylus fulvicephalus*, which has spotted wings.

Most brown lacewing larvae feed on aphids, but they are slimmer and less bristly than those of the green lacewings, and never camouflage themselves with aphid skins or other debris. Giant lacewing larvae live in wet moss and debris at the edges of streams. Species of *Sisyra*, commonly known as sponge flies, also live near streams, where their larvae feed inside freshwater sponges.

Green lacewings lay numerous eggs on the underside of leaves where aphids are found. Long, delicate stalks of hardened mucus help to protect the eggs from predators.

WILDLIFE WATCH

Where can I find lacewings?

● The common green lacewing frequently passes the winter months hibernating in houses.

● Look among dead leaves and under bark or logs for the white cocoons in which most lacewings spend the winter.

● Green and brown lacewings are widely distributed but are most common in the south. They are on the wing from early spring until well into the autumn.

● Gently search aphid-infested plants for lacewing larvae and for the stalked eggs of the green lacewings.

The giant lacewing, the largest British species, has distinctively spotted wings and a reddish or brown head. It can often be found resting by day on the foliage of trees in waterside gardens.

Winter garden moths

During the coldest months of the year, when predatory bats are hibernating, a number of hardy moths visit gardens to mate and lay their eggs so their caterpillars can enjoy the first foliage of spring.

Around 20 species of adult moths brave the chilly weather and fly during the winter months but most die long before the cold sets in. The vast majority of more than 2000 species found in Britain spend the winter as caterpillars, or eggs, while the adults of around 120 species survive by hibernating. However, the aptly named November moth, December moth, March moth, spring usher and winter moth are among those on the wing between October and March, when, even on the coldest nights, these moths are frequent visitors to gardens.

Safe season

It is surprising that any moths venture out at this time of the year at all. Winter nights are usually cold and damp, and very few flowers are in bloom to provide food in the form of nectar. However, there are advantages to flying during the winter months. One of these is that few predators are active. Bats, the main night-time predators of moths, are usually in hibernation, emerging in only small numbers to hunt them on occasional unseasonably warm nights.

The lack of nectar-bearing flowers does not bother many winter-flying moths, because most of them have no functional mouthparts and are therefore unable to feed. This is not as bizarre as it sounds, since these moths do all their feeding and growing while they are caterpillars, and

Sombre, sooty-black wings help the December moth blend in with the winter colours of tree bark and fungi as it rests during the hours of daylight.

◄ The male mottled umber moth is on the wing from dusk to dawn in parks and gardens all through the winter. During the day it rests on tree bark, perfectly camouflaged from marauding predators.

build up energy stores that they can draw upon as adults after pupation. The sole purpose of the adult stage of their life is to mate and reproduce, and once they have achieved this, they die.

Winter-flying moths are generally rather drab – most are a shade of brown or grey – and they have various biochemical and physiological adaptations that help them to survive freezing temperatures. Their body fluids generally contain large quantities of dissolved salts, as well as glycerol and similar anti-freeze compounds, which stop them freezing and dying even if the air temperature falls to –20°C (–4°F).

They can fly in freezing conditions because their wing muscles are able to work at lower temperatures than those of other moths. Despite this, the females of several species, such as the winter moth and mottled umber, are either wingless or have stunted wings that cannot be used to fly. Flying uses a lot of energy, especially in cold weather, and by not flying, these females have more energy to invest in producing eggs. After emerging from pupation in the ground, the wingless females crawl up trees and wait for the flying males to find them.

Winter visitors

Among the first moths to appear in winter is the December moth, which flies from October to January. It is somewhat stouter than most winter-flying species and its body has a thick furry coat. Both sexes are fully winged and the males fly quite rapidly, even in frosty weather. The sprawler moth appears soon after, flying from late October to early December. Both males and females can fly, and they are often seen on window panes.

True to its name, the November moth is most frequently seen in November, although it appears earlier in the north where it can be sighted at any time between mid-September and the end of November. Its forewings are dull grey or buff, usually with paler bands, although these are not always very obvious. Both sexes can fly.

The female mottled umber moth is flightless and rarely seen, but the male flies in late autumn and often survives into January and February. Its forewings are usually some shade of brown with an irregular pale band through the centre and small dark dots around the outer edge. The wings are very variable. Those of some individuals are uniformly rich golden brown, while those of others are golden brown with a dark wavy line and dark spot.

Winter moth females are also wingless, but the males have drab brown wings and fly from October to January. This moth is one of the most common winter visitors to gardens throughout Britain.

Daytime camouflage

During the daytime all these moths hide in the vegetation, or roost on tree trunks and fences. Many are amazingly well camouflaged when at rest, with an instinct for choosing backgrounds that match their coloration. They flatten their wings against the surface to eliminate any shadows that might betray their shape. Although they may take to the wing when disturbed in daytime, they are fully active only at night.

WINTER GARDEN

JANUARY • FEBRUARY

The male mottled umber often comes to lighted windows, distracted from its search for a female. Its caterpillars can be serious pests in orchards, but are rarely a problem in gardens.

Another mid-winter moth is the angle shades. Its larvae eat various herbaceous plants, and as a result they are often brought indoors in the autumn along with potted geraniums. They then pupate, and the adults appear in the house in winter.

◄ At a glance, the angle shades moth is easily mistaken for a dead leaf. It flies throughout the winter, while in autumn its numbers are swelled by immigrant angle shades moths from the Continent.

► On mild winter nights, mottled umber moths are sometimes attracted to outdoor lights. These are all males, because the females are wingless and are found only on the trees where they breed.

JULY • AUGUST

If disturbed in the daytime, the large yellow underwing launches into a fast and erratic flight, flashing its bright yellow hind wings and then dropping quickly back to the ground where it is hard to spot. Its caterpillars are known as cut-worms, because they feed at night on the stems of young plants.

The swallowtailed moth appears ghost-like during its dusk flights. It is often attracted to lighted windows.

▲ Large yellow underwings are often disturbed from herbaceous borders and vegetable plots during the day.

► Not to be confused with the very rare swallowtail butterfly, the swallowtailed moth is a frequent garden visitor during the summer.

MOTH CALENDAR

MARCH • APRIL

Male March moths are readily attracted to light and can sometimes be found by torchlight, resting on fruit trees in the garden. A close look will often reveal one of the spider-like, wingless females nearby on the trunk.

Like many moths the Hebrew character holds its wings in a tent-like fashion at rest, and can be recognised by the black 'bow-tie' markings on a grey or reddish-brown background.

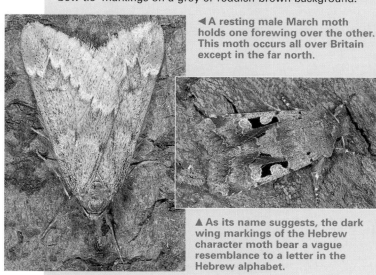

◄ A resting male March moth holds one forewing over the other. This moth occurs all over Britain except in the far north.

▲ As its name suggests, the dark wing markings of the Hebrew character moth bear a vague resemblance to a letter in the Hebrew alphabet.

MAY • JUNE

A giant compared to most other moths that occur in gardens, a privet hawkmoth is always an exciting find. Its handsome caterpillars feed on lilac and ash as well as privet.

In complete contrast, the white plume is a small, delicate moth, with wings divided into feathery plumes.

The magnificent privet hawkmoth is one of the most spectacular moths to be found on a regular basis in British gardens.

SEPTEMBER • OCTOBER

In common with many other autumnal moths, the pink-barred sallow often drinks the juices of over-ripe blackberries and other fruits and the nectar of ivy flowers. It is effectively camouflaged when resting on the ground among freshly fallen leaves.

The silver Y moth, named after the Y-shaped mark on each front wing, flies by day and night, but is usually seen as a greyish blur sipping nectar from flowers. This species may be active in winter.

► The attractive pink-barred sallow moth is often found on shrubby willow trees.

◄ The migrant silver Y is a summer visitor to Britain, arriving each year from southern Europe. It is often active by day, when it can be seen feeding from flowers.

NOVEMBER • DECEMBER

Winter moth males are active from dusk onwards on mild evenings. They seek wingless females, which wait hidden on the branches of trees and shrubs.

The November moth looks similar, but both males and females can fly. They are attracted to lights and may be found resting on shady house walls during the day.

▲ Only male winter moths have wings, which they use to seek out flightless females.

◄ November moths are exquisitely camouflaged when resting on bark.

FLIGHTLESS FEMALES

Most of the moths that are active in winter belong to the family Geometridae, and flightless females are common. Remaining sedentary is a strategy for concentrating scarce energy resources on producing eggs, at a time of year when low temperatures make flight difficult, and food is not available.

With either tiny flaps or no wings at all, the flightless females look more like spiders than moths, although they have only six legs. They emerge from their pupae in the ground or in bark crevices, and then crawl up the trunks of trees to wait for a mate. The males fly quite slowly in search of females, and have just enough spare energy to mate. In gardens, many are distracted by the lighted windows of nearby houses, and may cling to window panes for hours in the evenings.

The male winter moth is one of the most common of these night visitors. It often flies in the rain as well as on frosty nights. Meanwhile the female sits on a deciduous tree – often an apple tree – waiting for a male to arrive. While mating they make a peculiar pair, with the male hanging upside down beneath the female, and this makes them easy to spot by torchlight. The pair may remain together for up to an hour before the male flies off.

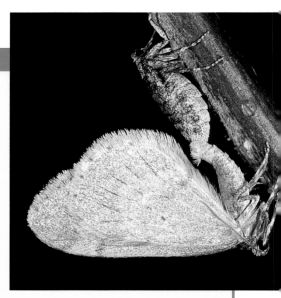

◀ Having mated with, and parted from, the male, the female winter moth crawls along the branches and twigs until she reaches the budding tips, where she lays her eggs. The caterpillars that hatch from the eggs feed on the young foliage.

▲ The pale wings of the male winter moth show up well in torchlight on winter evenings. A closer look will often reveal the bulkier female clinging to the branch above him. The male dies soon after mating, his job done.

Vital foodplants

Although the adult moths do not feed, they can be encouraged into the garden by providing the right kinds of foodplants for their caterpillars. These do little else but feed on plant tissues, usually leaves. With a few exceptions, each species of caterpillar is restricted to just a few related foodplants, so the greater the variety of plants in the garden, the more moths there are likely to be in residence. Trees, shrubs and hedges are especially important in this respect. Hawthorn, goat willow, poplar, birch, and apple all feed a wide range of moths.

Some caterpillars are voracious feeders. Those of the winter moth, for example, can destroy the spring foliage of apple trees. The wingless females can be deterred from climbing the trees by putting bands that have been treated with grease around the tree trunks. Avoid using chemical sprays, because these will kill all insects indiscriminately, including those that are harmless or beneficial species and bring life and interest to the garden, even in winter.

▲ Bold coloration warns birds and other predators that the magpie moth caterpillar has an unpleasant taste.

▼ From late December to March, illuminated windows often attract the pale brindled beauty. Those with wings are all males, in search of females. Their markings provide superb camouflage by day.

WILDLIFE WATCH

How can I see moths in winter?

● Since winter-flying moths do not feed – and there are few flowers for them to visit, anyway – their movements can be hard to predict. Many of the common winter-flying species become active just after dark, so use a torch to inspect fruit trees and native deciduous shrubs in the garden.

● They are often attracted to lighted windows and outside lights, so look on nearby walls.

● Shining a strong torch on to a white sheet left hanging from a washing line may lure the moths into settling on the sheet.

● When observing moths, try to identify them and make notes of when and where they appeared in the garden in order to keep a personal record.

Winter garden shrubs

A woodland grove or country hedgerow can be recreated in the garden with the help of native shrubs. During the winter months, such a refuge will shelter and succour wildlife great and small.

During cold, windy, snowy or icy weather, cosy nests and good roosting sites can mean the difference between survival and death for many mammals and birds. Carefully chosen shrubs not only offer shelter, but also sustenance through the winter months. When food is in the shortest supply, the fruit or nectar from late or early flowers benefits mice, squirrels and a whole host of birds, including winter visitors such as redwings, fieldfares and perhaps even scarce migrant waxwings. Butterflies, moths and other insects emerging early from hibernation can also share this source of nourishment.

Welcome visitors

A multitude of insects, spiders and other invertebrates are attracted to native species of shrubs. The vast majority of these visitors are harmless, or even beneficial to the plant and soil, and provide vital food for other creatures throughout the year, from dragonflies and frogs to wrens and blackbirds. Some 150 species of insects – nearly half of them moths – are associated with hawthorn, including bees, sawflies, beetles and leaf-hoppers. Blackthorn can sustain more than 100 insect species and hazel more than 70.

The sharp spikes of the hawthorn, blackthorn and wild roses (as well as cultivated pyracanthus and berberis) deter cats and other predators. The thorns make these shrubs a haven for nesting birds, while the hawthorn's striking crimson fruits, or haws, provide a winter feast. The fruits of the blackthorn, called sloes, resemble small plums and have a bluish bloom that wears off to reveal shiny black skin. Despite being mouth-numbingly tart to the human palate, sloes are eagerly devoured by birds such as thrushes, robins and starlings throughout autumn and winter. Masses of beautiful white flowers appear on the blackthorn as early as late March, a month before the similar, fragrant flowers of hawthorn, and provide early nectar for emerging insects.

Dogwood is justly renowned for the gorgeous glowing crimson colour of its stems in winter. In spring the leaves provide food for the caterpillars of various species of moths and for the green hairstreak and holly blue butterflies.

In summer, clusters of small, creamy white flowers produce plenty of nectar for insects, while from September into early winter, the black, pea-sized fruit attracts many birds.

Three species of native roses – dog rose, field rose and burnet rose – make delightful additions to any garden. Dog rose fruits later than the others, producing a winter supply of rosehips for hungry birds and rodents. Thrushes eat the smooth oval fruits whole, but smaller birds, especially greenfinches, and wood mice remove the seeds.

▲ **Dogwood not only makes a fine, glowing display in the winter garden but also is of year-round benefit to a great variety of wildlife.**

The guelder rose, a member of the honeysuckle family, produces red, shiny berries that sustain birds, especially song thrushes, through the winter, while the bullfinch relishes the flattened seeds, one inside each fruit.

The crab-apple (a small tree rather than a shrub) bears fruit that, unlike that of most cultivated apple trees, remains on

▲ The small oval hips of the field rose are, like those of other species of native British wild roses, devoured by birds, mice and other wildlife.

▶ Scarlet autumn leaves on the guelder rose, a wild member of the honeysuckle family, find an echo in the shiny red berries of this handsome shrub.

▼ Hips produced by the dog rose are larger and more elongated than those of the field rose. They appear in August and often last well into winter.

the ground in good condition throughout the winter. These miniature apples are valued in the early months of the year – great tits and chaffinches peck out the seeds while thrushes, crows, starlings and little muntjac deer eat the flesh.

Garden birds also relish spindle, an attractive, fast-growing shrub with toothed leaves that turn a beautiful pinkish red colour in autumn. This is when the bright coral-pink four-lobed fruits split to reveal in each lobe a single seed enclosed (like the seeds of yew) in a fleshy, berry-like structure called an aril, which is bright orange. The flesh is more rich in nutrients than any other native fruit, with

a high proportion of fats and proteins and a low water content. Robins are so fond of it that an old country name for the spindle fruit was 'robin's bread'. The seeds are avoided by birds and other wildlife, and are poisonous to humans. Caterpillars of the holly blue butterflies eat the spring buds of the spindle while the small white flowers are rich in nectar, attracting butterflies and other insects in spring and early summer.

Berries and flowers

Holly is one of the most valuable native winter shrubs. Its tough, glossy, prickly, evergreen leaves provide excellent cover

for birds all year round, while the familiar red berries are relished by thrushes, blackcaps, wood pigeons and other birds in the depths of winter when most other fruit is scarce. Holly blue caterpillars and leaf-miners feed on the buds in spring. Regular clipping can prevent fruiting, so

HEDGES AND CLIMBERS

Shrubs can be used to create or improve boundaries, both those separating the property from neighbours and – if it is large enough – within the garden, to delineate areas such as a vegetable patch, or to screen unsightly compost bins or fuel bunkers. Hedges are not that difficult to establish. They are far easier to maintain over time than wooden fences or stone walls, and concentrate plenty of wildlife in a limited space.

Privet is one of the archetypal hedging plants, with the bonus of withstanding pollution in town gardens, but choose the native wild species (*Ligustrum vulgare*) and not the cultivated Japanese species *Ligustrum ovalifolium*, because the latter is of little value to wildlife. The blackish stems of blackthorn have even fiercer thorns than hawthorn, making it a good choice for a boundary hedge.

A mixed hedge, such as two-thirds hawthorn combined with about a fifth field maple and smaller amounts of wild privet, holly, dog rose, guelder rose and dogwood, can produce an interesting display. Plant

the shrubs about 45cm (18in) apart. A staggered double row will yield a thicker hedge than planting a single row. Remove the upper third of their shoots after planting to encourage dense branching.

Climbing shrubs, including native honeysuckle (*Lonicera periclymenum*) and old man's beard or traveller's joy (*Clematis vitalba*), trained against walls or fences, or even up a tree or other shrub, are especially valuable in small gardens, because they take up very little space on the ground. They provide not only food in the form of nectar, fruit and seeds but also shelter for birds, insects and other wildlife. For this reason, train the shrubs to grow up netting or wires attached to blocks fitted at intervals to the wall or fence, so that they stand about 10cm (4in) away from the boundary. This will create a shady space for various creatures to hide in safety.

The clusters of black berries of wild privet, a semi-evergreen relative of the olive tree, are devoured by many birds, especially blackbirds, but are poisonous to humans.

▲ Most holly berries are bright red in colour but some varieties of the plant produce yellow or golden ones, and may also have variegated leaves.

ESSENTIAL IVY

Ivy is an exceptionally useful plant for the wildlife-friendly garden, of year-round importance since it is evergreen. It is very easy to grow in almost any situation, but prefers shade and a fairly rich soil. It needs no tying-in because its shoots bear tiny aerial roots that cling tenaciously to vertical surfaces. As well as providing dense cover for nesting birds, it also shelters hibernating butterflies, moths and other insects, and perhaps even a few bats. Its small yellowish flowers last long into the winter, providing nectar for late-flying insects, while in most years the clusters of fruits do not ripen to their deep purplish black colour until late winter. They provide much-needed food for birds and animals at a time of year when most other fruits, such as hips and haws, have already been devoured. Ivy fruit are appreciated by winter visitors such as redwings and fieldfares, as well as by larger birds, especially wood pigeons.

An attractively variegated ivy turns a plain wall into a beautiful screen that provides food, shelter and nest sites for a whole range of garden wildlife.

for attracting birds – and making Christmas decorations — it is better grown as a small tree. Male and female flowers grow on separate trees, and only females produce berries.

From January onwards, the appearance of yellow 'lambs' tails' catkins of hazel brighten up the garden. These are the male flowers of the only nut-bearing tree native to Britain. A little later, but before the leaves appear, the female flowers open. Bursting with pollen and full of sweet nectar, these succour a host of insects, including early bumblebees. The nuts ripen in autumn and often remain where they fall well into winter. These are eagerly sought by squirrels, mice and other rodents, as well as nuthatches and woodpeckers. The delightfully named long-snouted nut weevil lays its eggs in the hazelnut, and the resulting larvae bore their way out to pupate on the ground.

Cultivation tips

Berries and fruits of native shrubs appear at varying times of the year, so growing an assortment of them can sustain wildlife throughout the autumn and winter. Plant some so that the fascinating comings and goings of animals and birds can be seen from the house, but take care not to site them where cats can hide and pounce without warning.

It is important, too, not to prune and trim overzealously. Allowing shrubs to mature and grow to 3m (10ft) or more will give both the wildlife and the garden

▶ Although some sloes on a blackthorn bush may shrivel and wither after just a few weeks, most remain to provide a feast for birds until late winter.

privacy and prevent neighbours, or noisy traffic on an adjacent roadway or pavement, from causing a disturbance — as well as reducing pollution.

Decay is a vital part of the natural cycle and of great value to fungi, woodlice, millipedes, snails, slugs and wood-boring insects, all of which obtain food from the rotting wood. These in turn provide food for toads, frogs, hedgehogs and birds. For this reason, try to retain some dead wood as far as possible.

Resist the urge to tidy up by sweeping away dead leaves from beneath shrubs. Allowing the leaves to remain where they fall will produce a ground layer of leaf

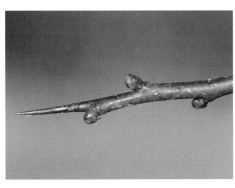

▲ The sharp spines of hawthorn are borne at the ends of branches as well as at intervals along their length.

▲ The coral pink fruits of the spindle produce seeds that feed many birds, especially robins.

▶ A spindle in November is a flaming beauty. The leaves turn an intense deep pinkish red in autumn.

litter among which dunnocks, blackbirds, song thrushes, robins and other birds, as well as mice, voles, foxes and other mammals can search for food through autumn and winter. The leaves form a natural mulch that keeps the soil moist and warm. In time, all the leaves, except tough, leathery ones such as those of holly, will rot down into a rich layer of leaf mould that will add valuable humus to the soil.

Another bonus of growing shrubs in the garden is that they provide shade for some of the native wild flowers found in hedgerows and on woodland edges, which will attract insects and other animals. Wood anemones, primroses, violets, red campion, herb Robert, white dead-nettle and wild strawberries are just some of the beautiful plants that you can sow in the garden, or that may even spring up naturally.

WILDLIFE WATCH

How can I grow winter shrubs in the garden?

● For the quickest and most reliable results, buy shrubs ready for planting from a reputable garden centre or mail-order supplier. For less common species, you may need to contact a specialist nursery. (Look through advertisements in gardening magazines.)

● Dig a hole for each shrub that is wider and deeper than its root ball. When inserting bare-rooted specimens, gently spread out the roots around the hole. Container-grown ones should simply be tapped out of their pot, leaving plenty of compost surrounding the roots. Mix the soil removed when digging the hole with a couple of handfuls of bonemeal, then use this compound to fill in around the roots of the shrub. Shaking the trunk gently removes any air pockets that may prevent

the fine root hairs from absorbing food and water. Plant at the correct depth – place the shrub too deep and the trunk may rot. Ensure that the top of the compost is level with the soil surface after firming-in plants grown in containers; with bare-rooted ones, the soil mark on the trunk should be level with the surface of the soil. Finally, after staking the shrub if it is large, give the surrounding soil a thorough watering.

● Although large container-grown specimens can be planted at any time of year to produce instant results, it is cheaper by far to purchase young, bare-rooted plants that have been grown by the supplier in the ground and are dug up just before you buy them. Bulk purchases can lead to considerable savings.

● It is important to prepare the planting site well in advance. To allow for spreading roots as the shrub grows, thoroughly dig the soil over an area of several square metres and add humus in the form of garden compost or well-rotted manure throughout.

● The best time of year to plant most woody shrubs is either late autumn or early spring, provided the weather is not too cold or wet.

● The soil next to a wall or fence is often dry, so prepare it for planting by adding extra compost or manure to keep the soil moist until the plants are well established. Plant climbers at least 30cm (1ft) away from the wall or fence, so that rain can reach the roots.

The holly tree

One of the most familiar trees of both garden and park, the vivid red berries of holly provide much-needed food for many creatures, especially birds. Large flocks descend to feast on the winter's crop.

A long with box, ivy and privet, holly is a broadleaved woody evergreen plant, native to the British Isles. Other native woody evergreens include yew, juniper and Scots pine but these are not broadleaved. Bushy and many-branched, holly has relatively smooth brownish grey bark and glossy, prickly leaves. It usually grows up to 15m (50ft) tall, but it can reach heights of almost 25m (80ft), developing a massive trunk and branches.

Holly has been used in winter religious rituals since historical records began. Not only were its leaves a potent symbol of life in mid-winter, but the berries were thought to ward off evil, like the red berries of another native tree, the rowan or mountain ash. In Ireland, holly is one of the trees associated with fairies. Christianity also adopted the symbolism, with the prickly leaves representing Christ's crown of thorns and the red berries his blood.

Fine timber

In the distant past, the holly's association with eternal life and its reputation for keeping evil at bay gave it semi-sacred status, and it was considered bad luck to cut down a holly

▲ **Only female holly trees bear berries, although all of them have white flowers. The flowers are not so sought after by birds as the berries, and have no traditional significance.**

tree. More recently these qualms have been overcome, and the tree is often felled for its extremely fine, pale, hard timber, which is particularly well suited for decorative carving or inlay work.

Another tradition associated with the holly tree is that a good crop of berries is a warning of a hard winter to come. In fact there is no basis for this belief, since a plentiful

▲ **Holly leaves have a tough waxy coat that resists decay. When they finally start to break down, the rigid structure of veins that maintained the leaf in life creates an inflexible, persistent skeleton in death.**

crop of berries is just a sign that the tree has enjoyed a good spring and summer. No tree can predict the nature of the seasons. It can only react to them as they occur.

HOLLY FACT FILE

A native evergreen tree, holly grows everywhere except on wet soils or in areas that suffer very cold winters with long frosty periods. It tolerates shade and often grows under oak or beech trees.

● **NAMES**
Common name: holly
Scientific name: *Ilex aquifolium*

● **HABITAT**
Woodlands, parks and gardens, farmland except on waterlogged soil

● **DISTRIBUTION**
Throughout the British Isles

● **HEIGHT**
Usually up to 15m (50ft), occasionally to around 25m (80ft)

● **LIFESPAN**
At least 400 years

● **BARK**
Smooth and green when young; greyish when mature, becoming warty with age

● **LEAVES**
Alternate on short stalks, dark green, leathery and mostly hairless, upper surface waxy and shiny, paler beneath, usually wavy; margins armed with sharp spines; remain on the tree for up to 4 years, still green when they fall; oval non-spiny leaves with pointed tips on higher branches

● **FLOWERS**
Male and female flowers on separate trees; small, white (sometimes purple-tipped) and waxy, each with 4, rarely 5 petals; scented; appear in dense clusters in May–August; nectar attracts bees and other pollinating insects

● **FRUITS**
Clusters of fleshy, spherical red berries, each enclosing 4 seeds – borne on female trees September–January

● **USES**
Ideal for hedging; wood pale and hard, good for decorative carving; burns well even when green; foliage still cut for feeding to livestock in some places

The narrow crown is usually conical, but older trees have flattish spreading crowns and become increasingly straggly.

The neat male flowers of the holly tree have four prominent yellow-headed stamens. Their pollen is collected by insects that transfer it to the female flowers in order to fertilise them.

The leaves are thick, with waxy surfaces that help them to resist water loss when the soil is frozen.

Where the tree is not browsed or trimmed, the lower branches become dense and spreading.

Female flowers develop into berries, which ripen by October. These are usually red, but sometimes orange or yellow. Variegated trees may be found in the wild.

▼ Browsing animals, such as deer, have a visible impact on holly trees, particularly during the winter months. They leave a distinct line, marking the highest point they can reach.

▲ The white flowers of both male and female holly trees grow in tight, showy clusters in the axils of the leaves. The individual flowers are about 6mm (¼in) across.

FEEDING FRENZY

Birds of the thrush family are particularly partial to holly berries. In autumn, resident blackbirds, song thrushes and mistle thrushes are a familiar sight in and around berry-bearing trees in gardens. But as winter approaches, and the holly berries ripen in quantity, the resident thrushes have to compete with an influx of winter-visiting relations – particularly redwings and fieldfares that have flown in from Scandinavia and other parts of northern and eastern continental Europe.

In an attempt to keep the berries for itself, an individual mistle thrush – or sometimes a pair – will often stake a claim to a particular holly tree or shrub. They repel all comers with loud calls and threatening displays. However, if the winter in Scandinavia is particularly harsh, making food hard to find, huge numbers of redwings and fieldfares will arrive in Britain. After exhausting crops of hawthorn berries, they descend on ripe holly bushes in large numbers. They are often joined by blackbirds and song thrushes, forming a mixed-species feeding flock that completely overwhelms the resident mistle thrush. In its attempts to drive them away it misses out on the ensuing free-for-all, and in less than a day the entire berry crop can be stripped from the tree.

Redwings gorge themselves on holly berries mainly in December and January. They feed in flocks, making short work of berry crops that might feed one bird for several weeks.

Edible foliage

Holly is highly nutritious for many animals and, more importantly, it is available at a time when they have little else to eat. It is thought that the spiny leaves evolved in an attempt to protect the tree from the ravages of browsing animals. Significantly, the most prickly leaves occur low on the tree, where they are accessible to large animals reaching up from ground level. Higher up the tree, beyond the reach of most browsers, the leaves are usually spineless.

However, despite the spines, deer, cattle and horses still eat the foliage, giving many holly trees a perfectly level line marking the highest point that the animals can reach, known as the browse line. In upland areas, where the grazing is relatively poor, holly foliage is so attractive to animals that the trees cannot thrive, and large specimens are restricted to inaccessible cliffs, ledges and boulder fields.

In some regions, such as parts of Shropshire, the foliage was traditionally cut to be fed to livestock. The prickly leaves were sometimes ground up using special machines to make them more palatable.

Seed dispersal

If the leaves of holly entice browsing mammals, it is the berries that generate the most excitement among birds. Their conspicuous colour is highly attractive to hungry birds and, in hard winters, they have been known to strip the trees bare.

Far from damaging the tree, this helps the holly to scatter its seeds. If the seeds fell to the ground directly below the tree, the saplings would have to grow in the deep shade cast by the parent tree's thick foliage, and would eventually compete with it for soil nutrients. So the tree relies on birds to carry off its seeds and eventually pass them, undamaged, in their droppings. The consequences of this can often be found beneath nearby trees, where holly grows from seeds contained in the droppings of perching birds. The seedlings

DID YOU KNOW?

In the Chilterns, holly was once known as 'Christmas tree', for obvious reasons. This probably explains the name of a local site called Christmas Common, where hollies are very numerous.

Holly makes an excellent year-round windbreak. Few large animals would attempt to break through its prickles. A mature female holly hedge provides secure shelter and abundant winter food for all kinds of wildlife.

begin life with two soft, deciduous seed leaves, followed by the normal spiny, evergreen foliage.

Thick holly bushes also make extremely good nesting sites for small birds. A variety of woodland and garden birds, including robins, blackbirds and some warblers will take advantage of the dense cover, which keeps off the worst of the weather and offers a degree of protection against crows and other thieves.

Insect life

Holly supports a number of insects. They include the caterpillars of the holly blue butterfly and those of two small moths, the double-striped pug and yellow-barred brindle. They all eat the flower buds and flowers, and the holly blue caterpillars eat the berries, too.

Close examination of a garden holly tree will often reveal ribbon-like tracks on its leaves. The blotchy trails are the work of the holly leaf-miner, the larva of a tiny fly. The miner lives in between the upper and lower surfaces of the leaf, and even pupates in this tiny space. The trails often end in ragged holes where the grubs have been

HOLLY BLUE BUTTERFLY

The attractive holly blue, marked with inky blue above, and silvery grey with black dots beneath, is by far the most common blue butterfly in gardens, and the species is a regular visitor to parks and gardens in England.

Uniquely among British butterflies, the caterpillars of the holly blue eat different foodplants depending on the season. There are two generations of the butterfly each year. In spring, the adult female lays its tiny eggs singly, each one on a holly flower bud or developing berry. The emerging caterpillars feed on

the flower buds, becoming butterflies in July. When their turn comes to breed in August, they lay their eggs on the flower buds of ivy.

These late broods overwinter as pupae, then emerge as adults in the spring to begin the cycle again. They can damage foodplants, but they themselves fall prey to an ichneumon wasp that lays eggs in their soft bodies.

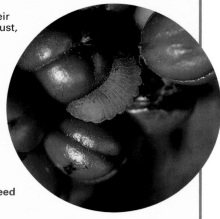

Holly blue caterpillars are well camouflaged as they feed on holly flower buds.

pecked out by small birds, and such is the complexity of insect life that the miner itself is sometimes parasitised by a minute wasp.

On sunny summer days holly trees may be surrounded by clouds of tiny white flying insects called psocids – relatives of booklice – buzzing around the leaves. Little is known about their habits, but they probably feed on holly pollen, and on algae growing on the leaves. In this latter respect, they may perform a valuable service to the tree, cleaning up its foliage so it functions more efficiently.

▼ **A holly seedling has rooted in the rotting stump of a dead tree. Sturdy seedlings often spring up in surprising places – seeds passed in bird droppings sprout where they fall.**

▶ **An almost impenetrable barrier of spiny leaves makes a holly tree an ideal nest site for small birds. Here the foliage helps to keep a brood of young blackcaps safe from harm.**

WILDLIFE WATCH

Where can I see holly trees?

● The mixed woodland of holly and pollarded oak at Staverton in Suffolk contains a holly tree 23m (75ft) tall, with a 2.2m (7ft) girth – one of the largest hollies in Britain.

● Pure holly woods are unique to Britain. The most remarkable is a dwarf holly wood on the great coastal shingle headland of Dungeness in Kent.

● Clusters of hollies close to grazing pasture, known as hollins, were once harvested for foliage to feed to livestock. The practice is now much less common, but old hollins can still be found, particularly in

Herefordshire, Shropshire, Staffordshire and north into the Pennines. To see hollins that are still in use, visit the New Forest, where boughs are still cut for cattle and ponies.

● Excessive grazing pressure means that the New Forest is one of the best places in the country to see browse lines on holly trees. Despite this, holly is more abundant here than in most other forests.

● Several place names are thought to be derived from holly, or from 'holm', 'hulver' or 'holegn' – which became 'hollin' – all old English names for the species.

Park watch

- Watching squirrels
- Recognising deer
- The tawny owl
- Recognising thrushes
- The green woodpecker
- The jay
- Ground beetles
- Recognising mosses and liverworts
- The mistletoe
- The yew tree

Watching squirrels

On cold, bright days, squirrels emerge from their quarters to forage for food. They can often be seen bounding through a park, or digging and searching for the nuts they buried in the autumn.

ven in the depths of winter, squirrels are extremely active. They do not hibernate, as many people wrongly assume, and their behaviour gives ample opportunity to observe them in urban as well as rural settings on bright winter days.

Grey squirrels are plentiful all over the country. Their characteristic footprints are a common sight in a light snowfall. These familiar creatures provide much entertainment to anyone watching, especially their mating chases, which begin in January. Red squirrels, on the other hand, are a much rarer sight. Although they inhabit coniferous forests all over Scotland, hardly any live in the southern half of England, and experts fear that they may soon die out altogether in mainland England and Wales and in Ireland.

Finding food

Winter is the hardest season for many wild animals, but squirrels actually reach their maximum weight in January, just before they start to breed. Even so, finding enough food is a challenge. Nuts and fruit have fallen from the trees and strong winds make climbing and leaping among branches a risky business. Also, the days are very short – a particular problem for red squirrels, which need more than eight hours a day to gather enough food to survive. Overcast winter days provide them with barely enough daylight. The problems are worse when bad weather delays the onset of spring. Winter may be lengthened by more than a month and many squirrels, especially the younger ones, struggle to cope.

Grey squirrels seem capable of finding sufficient nourishment in less time than reds, perhaps because they eat more food that is available on the ground. Red squirrels feed mostly in the treetops, where food is scarce and widely scattered. At this time of year, red squirrels search for a fungus called *Vuilleminia*, which grows as a thin pinkish or buff crust under the bark of dead or dying oak branches, but it is not very nutritious.

Even in extreme cold, the red squirrel must forage, because it cannot go for more than a few days without food.

Aggression is rife in late winter as grey squirrels vie for mates and territories. Fights break out regularly and rivals crash around in the canopy or undergrowth, chattering in fury, oblivious to watching humans.

Nuts are a staple food for many months of the year, from autumn onwards. Squirrels, especially greys, waste no time in exploiting a crop, often beginning to eat the nuts before they are fully ripe. Moreover, squirrels do not waste time on nuts that have already been damaged by insects. Weevils, for instance, may hollow out a hazelnut from inside, leaving an intact but empty shell. This nut is then of no use either to the tree or the squirrel. If a squirrel picks up a nut that weighs little, indicating that it is empty, it quickly drops the shell again. Only good, heavy nuts will be carried away and stored. In this way, squirrels ensure that food that could be seasonal is available to them for as long as possible – often until early spring.

Winter larder

A squirrel does not remember the exact location of specific food items – it only recalls the general area of the cache. Since several squirrels often use the same prominent landmarks as signposts for their caches, large numbers of nuts, acorns and other useful foodstuffs are frequently buried in the same patch of ground. When digging up food later on, a squirrel is just as likely to find food buried by another individual as it is its own hoard. It might also unearth other snacks, such as insect larvae, buried in the soil.

Some buried nuts are never found, and this is one way in which the seeds of trees are scattered and planted. So while squirrels eat many of the acorns an oak tree produces, if just one buried acorn germinates to grow into a new tree, this is a mutually beneficial partnership.

A squirrel's success over the winter depends very much on its activities during the preceding autumn. If food is

abundant, squirrels eat as much as they can as well as burying large stores of acorns and nuts for use later on. This helps the animals to accumulate plenty of fat beneath the skin and around their internal organs. These fat reserves not only provide insulation against the cold, but also act as vital emergency rations when deep snow or very bad weather means that the squirrels cannot come out to feed. Their fat also enables squirrels to survive the long, dark nights and gloomy days when there are not enough daylight hours for them to gather sufficient food.

Fat reserves

Grey squirrels have a big advantage over reds in being able to lay down much larger fat reserves. Indeed, in winter, greys can look decidedly chubby. Too much weight is not a problem for them because they do most of their foraging on the ground, where lightness and agility are not crucial. Red squirrels, however, depend on remaining athletic and fully agile in the branches where they feed.

In conifer forests, red squirrels feed on the seeds in pine cones. These are available all year round, but are widely spaced and located at the tips of thin branches. The squirrels simply cannot afford to get fat because this would make leaping about among the branches dangerous, difficult and tiring.

It is because they carry less fat that red squirrels are more vulnerable to starvation than greys when the winter drags on for a few extra weeks, or when prolonged periods of bad weather stop them from feeding properly.

In some years, trees produce particularly bountiful crops of nuts and acorns. These are called 'mast years' and are good times for squirrels, enabling

SECRET STASH

One way that both red and grey squirrels manage to overcome the difficulty of food shortages in winter is to store food from the previous autumn. They collect nuts and other seasonal foods that will not easily decay, and hide them away. The hoarded cache can be dug up much later and can make the difference between survival and starvation.

▶ Squirrels tend to hide large numbers of food items within the same few areas, such as at the base of a big oak tree or in a patch of short grass. This behaviour is called 'scatter hoarding'.

◀ When the squirrel needs to draw on its food store, it will return to the area and dig about until it finds buried nuts. These can remain in good condition for several months in the soil, provided that they stay reasonably dry.

TREE HOUSES

Both red and grey squirrels prefer to sleep in well-lined tree holes, called dens. These may be natural or the abandoned nest-holes of woodpeckers. Grey squirrels in particular will often gather together to share a hole and build up a warm fug inside to help them all keep out the winter cold. Sometimes five or more animals may live together in this way.

Squirrels also build special nest-like homes, called dreys, in tree branches. It seems that greys at least choose different sites to build in winter and summer. Their summer dreys are often sited out among thin branches, amid the foliage and close to any flowers and fruit they may want to harvest from the tree canopy. However, after the leaves have fallen in the autumn, these dreys are fully exposed to wind and rain. In winter, the flimsy branches are tossed about by gales and the dreys are not very secure, so the squirrels build new ones. These are sited on large, sturdy branches and tucked up close to the main tree trunk. Here, they are stable in the face of high winds and are relatively sheltered from driving rain. Winter dreys and the remains of summer

▼ Red squirrels will occasionally make use of nestboxes put up for birds. This is an opportunity not available to greys because their larger frame means they are too big to enter standard boxes.

ones can often be seen, especially in late winter, when the benefits and drawbacks of their siting are usually obvious.

A seasonal change of nesting position is not a hard and fast rule, though. Red squirrels, more often than greys, nest in conifers where protective masses of needles are present throughout winter. It does not make much difference to them where their dreys are sited, so building a new one for winter is not necessary.

▲ The drey is a compact, spherical structure, about the size of a football, made of twigs and leaves. It is sited high in a tree.

▲ A grey squirrel may simply squeeze into a hollow tree or make its home in an old woodpecker hole.

them to face the winter in prime condition. In time, this enables the mothers to produce large litters and to nourish them more effectively. In poor mast years, squirrels have their work cut out just surviving, especially during prolonged spells of bad weather. They may still breed, but a mother with insufficient fat is unable to produce much milk, so she will not be able to raise all her young. Perhaps only one of the litter will survive.

Winter coat

Cold is obviously a problem for squirrels, especially as they do not enjoy the benefits of an insulated underground burrow system. Like many other mammals, they prepare for winter by moulting their sparse summer coat and growing dense new fur. To anyone watching squirrels regularly, this process is quite noticeable. It starts on the back and moves forwards and downwards, with the flanks and belly being last to change. While this change is in progress, there can be a striking difference between the fine, sleek fur at the front end of the animal and the thickly furred back legs – which creates the impression that the squirrel is wearing furry breeches.

In grey squirrels, the mainly reddish brown summer coat is replaced by hairs with prominent white tips, giving the winter coat a paler, silvery look and an overall grizzled appearance. The winter coat is at least twice as dense as the

Grey squirrels can look very chubby by late autumn, carrying perhaps 15 to 20 per cent more weight than usual in the form of fat. Such reserves are vital if the animal is to survive long periods of poor weather when it cannot feed.

Fighting fit

Despite the many and varied hardships that winter brings, by the new year squirrels have more than mere survival on their minds. Male red squirrels, resplendent with their long ear tufts, compete for territories and are constantly on the alert for intruders and potential rivals.

When on the ground, the squirrel often pauses to look around, rising up on its haunches and using its tail as a balance.

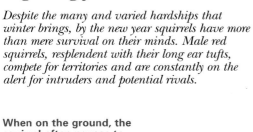

TRACKS IN THE SNOW

Squirrel footprints in a dusting of snow confirm that these creatures are very active during the winter. They often come out on fine days, even if there is snow on the ground. Squirrels usually move in a series of bounding leaps, which prevents them from getting too wet and cold. Tracks coming down from a tree are likely to be those of a squirrel. On the ground, the prints appear in groups of four about 25cm (10in) apart.

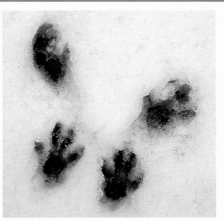

▲ In both red and grey squirrels, the hind paw prints have five toes. They appear in front of the much smaller forepaw tracks, which have only four toes.

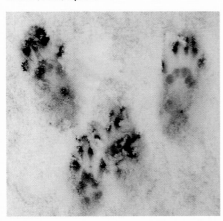

◄ Grey squirrel tracks are larger than those made by red squirrels. When bounding, greys place their hind feet in front of their forepaws, but when travelling fast they stay on their toes, which creates rounded prints.

The grey squirrel's short, thick winter fur repels water more readily than the red's, which makes grey squirrels far better suited to wet British winters. Reds are happiest in dry conditions – no matter how cold.

summer fur. It is moulted out again before the summer begins, first on the head and moving towards the rear.

Red squirrels also moult in preparation for winter. The winter hair is darker and longer than in summer, and makes the animal look quite chunky, as if wrapped up in an overcoat; their short summer fur makes red squirrels look far more streamlined. The new winter coat includes long ear tufts, which give the red squirrel a perky look. These are fully grown by January, but are lost in summer. They are not present at all in grey squirrels. Curiously, soon after the red squirrel's winter coat is fully grown the ear tufts and tail begin to bleach. Why this should happen is a mystery. There is no strong sunlight at this time of year and the

animals spend much of their time hidden away in nests. By about March, the ear tufts and tail are often cream.

Red squirrel hairs are very fine and provide excellent insulation. The animals survive well in eastern and northern Europe and Russia, where the winters are far more severe than in Britain. What they find much harder to cope with is mild, wet weather. Fine drizzle has a disastrous effect on their fur – the thin hairs swiftly become matted and lose their vital insulating properties. Red squirrels are highly prone to developing respiratory infections and losing body condition as a result of being wet. Grey squirrels, by contrast, with their shorter, thicker fur, can merely shake off most of the water if they get wet, and carry on feeding.

WILDLIFE WATCH

Where can I see squirrels in winter?

● Most parks have large numbers of grey squirrels. On bright winter days, they can be seen feeding greedily after days without food. Some are bold and may even take food from your hand. In wooded areas they can also be seen searching for the nuts that they have hoarded for winter.

● Squirrels willingly visit back gardens where nuts and scraps have been left out for the birds. They may also dig up tulip and crocus bulbs.

Recognising deer

Most of these naturally wary animals rarely venture far from cover and, if disturbed, will quickly disappear from sight. Taking note of their different antler shapes and markings on their rumps can assist in identification.

Deer are Britain's largest land mammals and are quite widely distributed. Even so, patience and stealth are needed to gain more than just a fleeting glimpse in the wild.

Red and roe deer were originally native to Britain but the current populations are mostly the result of reintroductions from Europe. Fallow deer, introduced by the Normans from the Continent about 800 years ago, have been established for so long that they are sometimes accepted as native.

Japanese sika deer are relative newcomers. They were introduced to several parks in the latter part of the 19th century and subsequently gave rise to wild populations. In Scotland, Ireland and the Lake District, sika and red deer have interbred, resulting in genetically mixed herds, and threatening the survival of the native red deer.

Two more recent arrivals are Reeves' (or Chinese) muntjac and the Chinese water deer. Both were among the many types of deer kept at Woburn Park early in the 20th century. Since then, releases and escapes of both species from various locations have resulted in wild herds.

Antler facts

Deer in the British Isles vary in size from the muntjac, about the size of a Labrador dog, to the cattle-sized red deer and reindeer, but they share several features. Almost all adult males of the deer family, or *Cervidae*, grow and shed a pair of antlers every year. Antlers are different from the horns of cattle or sheep, which are permanent bony structures covered with a layer of protein (keratin). Horns are common to both sexes.

Antlers consist of dense and very solid bone and grow to various sizes, depending on the species. The exception is the Chinese water deer, which does not grow antlers at all.

While growing, antlers are covered in 'velvet' – hairy skin containing blood vessels and nerves. This is rubbed off to expose bare bone when the antlers reach their full size for that year. The deer is then said to be in 'hard antler'.

Feeding and digestion

The daily eating patterns of deer alternate between bouts of foraging and chewing. Foliage, from hawthorn or bramble for instance, is bitten off by the lower front teeth pressing against a pad of hard tissue. Deer have no upper front teeth.

The food passes to the rumen, the first and largest compartment of the four-chambered stomach. Later it is regurgitated, a mouthful at a time, to be thoroughly ground down by the cheek teeth. It is then swallowed again, this time passing on to the other stomach chambers and through the gut, where vast numbers of micro-organisms break down the tough cellulose cell walls.

Sika deer are easier to see in winter when most of the undergrowth has died down and they come out into the open to feed.

EASY GUIDE TO SPOTTING DEER

Fallow deer — The antlers are typically broad and flat, a shape described as 'palmate'.

The horseshoe mark around the rump and line down the tail are black in the common colour variety, but brown in the menil form. There are no such markings in the black or the white colour varieties.

Red deer — The antlers are round in cross section, but bigger with more branching than those of the sika.

The rump patch is cream and the tail buff with no black. Both sexes have the same rump pattern.

Sika deer — The antlers are round in cross section.

The white heart-shaped rump patch is flared out like a powder puff when the deer is alarmed. The tail has a black line of variable width down at least part of its length.

Roe deer — The antlers are short and spiky, with a crusty look to the bases.

The rump patch, an inverted heart in females, kidney-shaped in males, is white in winter, cream-buff in summer. The white spike that looks like a tail is actually a tuft of hair called the anal tush.

Chinese water deer — Wide rounded ears and the males' long, curving, tusk-like upper canine teeth characterise the species.

The rump and stumpy tail are a similar yellowish colour to the body.

Reeves' muntjac — The antlers are tiny and do not have prongs. The bases are bony and very long. Males have short, tusk-like upper canine teeth.

The rump is unpatterned. The tail, a rich chestnut above, is held erect when the deer runs off in alarm, showing the white underside.

HOW CAN I IDENTIFY DEER?

● Look at the antlers – the form is distinctive for each species but there is individual variation and each pair of antlers differs from the previous set, with each set being bigger and more complex than the last.
• The first antlers of the red and fallow deer are simple spikes, very different from the ornate branched antlers of an old red stag or the broad, flattened antlers of a mature fallow buck.
• A sika's first antlers are single spikes, but even an old stag has just four points – or 'tines' – per antler.
• Roe deer antlers are short, seldom more than 25cm (10in), upright, and with a maximum of three points – forked at the top with one lower point. The main shaft is rough and knobbly.
• Muntjac antlers rarely exceed 8cm (3in).
• Chinese water deer have no antlers at all.

● In many cases, the only view to be had of a deer is its retreating rear. Fortunately, rumps are one of the best recognition features. Note the shape of the rump patch and

whether it is white or cream. Does it have black edges, or a black line down the middle, or both?

● Note the animal's size and posture. Muntjac carry their hindquarters higher than their shoulders; other deer have a more level back.

● Look at the grouping. Red, sika and fallow deer form separate-sex groups of varying sizes for most of the year, but come together for the rutting season. Roe are mostly found alone, or in small family groups. Muntjac and Chinese water deer are usually solitary.

● Unlike other species, fallow deer come in various colours, so a herd of mixed colours can only be fallow deer. The *common* variety is rich brown with white spots in summer – these virtually disappear in winter when the coat is a dull greyish brown. The *menil* variety is a lighter brown; the spots remain distinct in winter and the line down the mid-back, tail and around the rump is brown rather than black (as in the common form).

The *black* variety has a glossy summer coat, becoming dull brown in winter. The *partial albino* is a sandy colour at birth, but becomes white over successive moults.

● All deer have cloven hooves, which leave a divided footprint – known as a 'slot' – on damp soil or snow. However, it's hard to identify a species from slots alone, although the dainty 3cm (1¼in) print of a muntjac could hardly be confused with the 8cm (3in) print of a red deer.

WHAT ARE DEER?

● Deer are mammals that belong to the family *Cervidae*. Seven species inhabit the British Isles, including the reindeer which was introduced to the Cairngorms more than 50 years ago.

● All deer produce firm, black, glossy, pellet-shaped droppings.

● Mating rituals of red, fallow and sika deer involve the autumn rut when males fight with rivals. Red stags roar, fallow bucks groan and sika stags whistle and 'blow raspberries'.

WILDLIFE WATCH

Where can I see deer?

● The Forestry Commission has public hides and organises deer-watching trips in several of its forests, including at Thetford in Norfolk and Grizedale in the Lake District.

● Do not approach stags during the rut because they can be aggressive.

● Deer parks are good places to watch fallow or red deer – some have sika deer, too.

Distribution map key

 Present all year round

 Not present

FALLOW DEER *Dama dama*

For many centuries, the fallow deer was the species most frequently kept in parks because of its beauty, grace and the excellence of its venison. Some herds are all one colour, but often common or black varieties predominate, with a few menil or white individuals. Mature antlers are flat with short prongs, unlike those of any other species.

Fallow deer are variable in colour. They can be rich brown with white spots (common form in summer), almost black, dull greyish brown (common form in winter) or light brown with white spots.

● SIZE
Height to shoulder, buck 90–95cm (3ft–3ft 2in), doe 70–85cm (2ft 4in–2ft 10in); length nose to rump, 160cm (5ft 3in)

● BREEDING
Rut late September–November; single fawn born June

● FOOD
Grass, herbs, leaves of most broad-leaved trees and shrubs, nuts and other fruits, root crops

● HABITAT
Prefer mosaic of woodland, meadow, pasture or arable fields

● DISTRIBUTION
Widespread populations often close to, or in, present or former parks

Coat can be spotted or plain, light or dark, in either sex

Buck has prominent tufted penis sheath

Does and bucks look alike in early spring when the bucks have lost their antlers

RED DEER *Cervus elaphus*

The largest British native deer, the red deer's name refers to the rich red-brown summer coat, which becomes thicker and a dull brown in winter when the stags also grow a mane. For much of the year, stags and hinds live apart in groups of fewer than 10, some in woodland, others on open hillsides, where they may gather in herds, sometimes over 500 strong.

With newly cleaned antlers – each with distinct white points to the prongs – this stag is prepared for the September rut. Red deer are common in deer parks, where they may browse all the leaves off the trees to a height of about 2m (7ft).

● SIZE
Height to shoulder, stags 110cm (3ft 6in), hinds 100cm (3ft 4in); length nose to rump 200cm (6ft 6in)

● BREEDING
Rut September–end October; single fawn born May–June

● FOOD
Varies greatly with habitat; shoots and leaves of deciduous trees and conifers, grasses, heather, bramble, ivy, ferns

● HABITAT
Primarily woodland, but largest populations on treeless open moorland; may be seen foraging on arable crops close to forest

● DISTRIBUTION
Abundant throughout Scotland, small but increasing populations in Ireland and England; not established in Wales

Muzzle is long in both sexes, but in winter longer fur makes the face look rounded

Adult fur is orange-brown with no spots

Stags develop a thick, protective neck and mane in time for the rut, which persists through the winter

SIKA DEER *Cervus nippon*

The summer coat of the sika is like that of common coloured fallow. Its antlers are similar to those of youngish red deer, but typically have a maximum of four points per antler. The stag's facial markings give it a rather cross, frowning expression. There is an oval patch of white hairs below the hocks. Sika are often more secretive than red deer.

● **SIZE**
Height to shoulder, stag 81–85cm (2ft 8in–2ft 10in), hind 72–74cm (2ft 5in–2ft 6in); length nose to rump 140cm (4ft 7in)

● **BREEDING**
Rut September–November, single calf born May–June

● **FOOD**
Grasses, heather, ivy, nuts, fungi, tree foliage

● **HABITAT**
Dense woodland (often coniferous plantations), close to open areas

● **DISTRIBUTION**
Large populations in Scotland and Ireland, scattered concentrations in England, especially the Lake District and the New Forest, not found in Wales

Sika deer usually have a spotted coat even as adults. Their rounded antlers, with prominent prongs, distinguish them from spotted fallow deer, which have flat antlers.

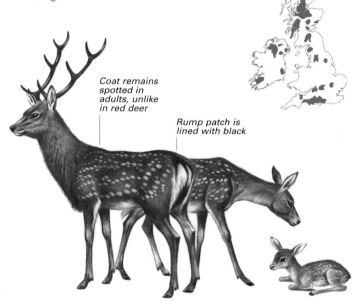

Coat remains spotted in adults, unlike in red deer

Rump patch is lined with black

ROE DEER *Capreolus capreolus*

Sleek reddish brown in summer, the roe deer is grey-brown in winter with or without two white patches on the throat. The white or cream rump is conspicuous, especially in winter against dead bracken or heather. Family parties may be spotted foraging in arable fields. If alarmed, they will bound away, giving gruff barks.

● **SIZE**
Height to shoulder, bucks and does similar, 63–67cm (2ft–2ft 3in); length nose to rump 105cm (3ft 6in)

● **BREEDING**
Rut July–August, single kid – sometimes twins, occasionally triplets – born May–June

● **FOOD**
Buds, shoots, leaves of trees and shrubs, bramble, ivy, heather, herbs, grasses

● **HABITAT**
Woodland, occasionally moorland; often in arable fields close to cover

● **DISTRIBUTION**
Throughout Scotland, northern England and across the Midlands, scattered colonies in the rest of England, not found in Wales and Ireland

Roe deer have short antlers, a white chin and a conspicuous, big neat area of black on the muzzle – other deer do not have such a large black nose. The pale rump patch never has any black markings. Roe are common, although because of their territorial habits they tend not to be kept in deer parks.

Bucks have short, knobbly antlers, often with only three points

Coat turns greyish brown from early October

Kid has conspicuous white spots on its dark brown coat, and a distinctive black 'moustache' on the upper lip

CHINESE WATER DEER *Hydropotes inermis*

In size and appearance, the Chinese water deer is somewhere between the roe and muntjac. The buck has no antlers, but he does have greatly elongated upper canine teeth that are used for fighting. These form large, curved tusks that protrude up to 7cm (2¾in) below the top lip, looking rather like a white moustache. The coat is reddish brown in summer and sandy in winter. The tail is never held erect.

● SIZE
Height to shoulder, buck 60cm (2ft), doe 50cm (1ft 8in); length nose to rump 95cm (3ft 2in)

● BREEDING
Rut from November–December, 2–3 fawns, occasionally more, born May–July

● FOOD
Grasses, sedges, rushes, deciduous shrubs and trees, herbs

● HABITAT
Extensive reedbeds, woodland and arable fields

● DISTRIBUTION
Mainly parts of Norfolk Broads, Fenlands of Cambridgeshire and Bedfordshire

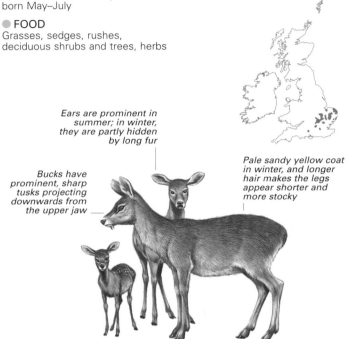

Ears are prominent in summer; in winter, they are partly hidden by long fur

Bucks have prominent, sharp tusks projecting downwards from the upper jaw

Pale sandy yellow coat in winter, and longer hair makes the legs appear shorter and more stocky

The Chinese water deer has beady black eyes and large sandy ears. It is common around parts of Bedfordshire and in Norfolk, but relatively scarce elsewhere. It prefers to live close to water.

REEVES' MUNTJAC *Muntiacus reevesi*

The muntjac is the smallest deer in Britain. Its coat is a glossy rich chestnut brown in summer and darker in winter. Muntjac are noisy, and may bark loudly and continuously, hundreds of times, over a 20 minute session or longer, especially during the rut. They have distinctive facial markings – the buck has black V-shaped stripes on the forehead, where the doe has a dark kite-shaped pattern.

● SIZE
Height to shoulder, buck and doe 43–52cm (1ft 5in–1ft 9in); length nose to rump 85cm (2ft 10in)

● BREEDING
Mating and birth of single fawn in any month; gestation averages 210 days

● FOOD
Buds, shoots, deciduous leaves, flowers, ivy, bramble, nuts, fungi, ferns

● HABITAT
Woodland with shrubby undergrowth, but also neglected cemeteries, gardens and overgrown embankments

● DISTRIBUTION
Well established in much of southern part of England, increasing colonies in rest of England and Wales, absent from Ireland

Antlers are backward pointing spikes

Tail has white underside

The doe is more slightly built than the buck

The muntjac is small and elusive, especially in its favoured dense woodland. It is about the size of a fox, and has a stocky body with raised hindquarters and humped back. Bucks have small tusks that protrude below the upper lip.

The tawny owl

A creature of the night, the big head and plump body of the tawny owl may sometimes be spotted silhouetted against the dark sky as it sits waiting for an unwary vole to venture into the open on the ground below.

Although some owls may be seen out hunting in daylight, the tawny owl is generally nocturnal. This makes it a difficult bird to observe, but it can often be heard, even during daylight hours. The tawny owl is highly vocal, especially in winter when boundaries are being established and birds are pairing up ready for mating.

The tawny has a large vocabulary of songs and calls. Ornithologists studying the sounds made by adults during the breeding season have identified 10 different calls, plus five calls made by the young. The most famous of the tawny owl's calls, usually written as '*tu-whit tu-who*' (by William Shakespeare among others), is really two calls, made by two birds. The '*tu-whit*' (or '*kewick*') is a contact call, most often made by the female, although the male also uses it. The '*tu-who*' (or '*hoo-hoo*') is the male's song, made both as a courtship and a territorial call, and when the male is bringing food for the female. During courtship the female and male call in rapid succession so that the '*tu-whit tu-who*' sounds like it comes from a single bird, when it's really a duet. Tawny owls call throughout the year, but not so often when the weather is cold, wet or windy, and during a full moon.

Night hunters

Tawny owls are found in wooded areas throughout most of Europe as far north as Scandinavia, as well as in North Africa and north and west Asia. In most places it hunts by night. However, in northern parts of Europe the summer nights are short – about four hours of darkness in northern Finland, for example – so tawnies can sometimes be seen hunting in the half-light of early morning. The other exception to the night-hunting rule is when the owls have a brood of owlets to feed. Then they may hunt later in the morning and earlier in the evening.

The tawny owl is a versatile hunter and uses an extensive repertoire of hunting strategies to catch small mammals. Its principal prey are the voles of its forest home, along with mice and shrews. Sitting quietly on a perch, the owl watches and listens for any activity below, swiftly dropping down to seize the prey in its talons. The owl kills the creature instantly by piercing it with its sharp hind claws.

Hunting on the wing is another of the owl's techniques. It takes birds from their roosts and sometimes beats bushes to startle small birds into flight. A tawny owl will even snatch incubating birds as big as blackbirds from off the nest. Insects such as beetles form a substantial part of its diet, as do numbers of earthworms and molluscs. If the owl is close to standing water, water shrews and frogs will be on the menu, too.

Tawny owls roost during the day but are seldom noticed because they are so superbly camouflaged. The plumage of British tawnies is a rich chestnut brown, beautifully streaked and speckled. The grey form is rarely seen in Britain. When a tawny owl is perched motionless on a branch, sitting close to the tree trunk with its silhouette concealed, it blends easily into the dappled woodland light. There, it spends most of the day dozing peacefully.

▲ During the day a tawny owl can doze quietly, tucked up against a tree trunk where its camouflage is most effective.

◄ At night, eyes wide open, the tawny owl sits on a convenient perch and scans the ground below, waiting for a small mammal to venture into the open.

BIG EYES

The eyes of a tawny owl are almost as large as those of a human. They are tubular rather than spherical, and so big that they cannot swivel in their sockets – instead the owl turns its whole head to look in a different direction.

The owl's ability to see at night is enhanced by the very large pupils of its eyes – almost twice the diameter of a human pupil. The large opening lets more of the available light into the eye, producing a brighter image on the retina. Its visual sensitivity is about 100 times that of a pigeon.

TAWNY OWL FACT FILE

These are the most common owls in Britain and both sexes look alike. Their legs and toes are feathered, providing some protection from the bites of mice and rats as they struggle to free themselves.

● NAMES
Common name: tawny owl
Scientific name: *Strix aluco*

● HABITAT
Woodland (especially old broad-leaved woods), wooded farmland, parks with trees, large gardens

● DISTRIBUTION
Widespread throughout England, Wales and Scotland; absent from Ireland, many Scottish islands and the Isle of Man

● STATUS
At least 20,000 breeding pairs in Britain

● SIZE
Length 37–39cm (14½–15½in); wingspan 81–96cm (32–38in); weight 350–500g (12–17½oz)

● KEY FEATURES
About the size of a woodpigeon; large head, stout body, streaked plumage, large black eyes; big broad wings and short tail

● HABITS
Flies and hunts at night, roosts during the day; solitary or in pairs, strongly territorial

● VOICE
Very vocal. Male has a long quavering hoot ('*hoo-hoo*' or '*hoo-hoo-hoo*'), both sexes make a '*kewick*' call, plus a range of other calls

● FOOD
Varied, chiefly small rodents, birds and insects

● BREEDING
Mid-March (though sometimes as early as late February) to mid-June; one brood

● NEST
Shallow, unlined hollows, mainly in holes in trees, old nests of larger birds, squirrel dreys, occasionally in old buildings and holes in the ground; readily accepts nestboxes

● EGGS
Usually lays a clutch of 2–4 white eggs, nearly round, at intervals; incubated by the female; hatch in 28–30 days

● YOUNG
Nestlings covered with thick white down; fledge in 32–37 days, but dependent on parents for food for up to 3 months after leaving the nest

● SIGNS
Irregularly shaped, grey pellets with bones of small mammal prey visible; found under a favourite perch

Distribution map key

■ Present all year round

□ Not present

The whole head swivels to enable the owl to see in another direction.

Large, round, dark eyes have very big pupils.

Mottled reddish brown, buff and dark brown plumage provides superb camouflage against tree bark and foliage.

Razor-sharp talons hold prey in a lethal grip.

Hunting senses

The tawny owl's night vision is as good as that of most other nocturnal animals, while its daytime vision is similar to that of a woodpigeon, which is active only by day. Hearing is the other sense most used for hunting and the tawny owl's large external ear openings enable it to hear many times better than other groups of birds, although its hearing ability is very similar to that of a keen-eared human.

The tawny owl's most remarkable feature is its excellent memory, which experiments have shown to be far better than that of most other birds and even superior to the recall of cats and dogs.

◄ The tawny owl's thick plumage helps to insulate the bird from the cold.

▼ Regular beats of its broad wings, interspersed with brief glides, give the tawny owl its fast, smooth flight.

A major reason why the tawny owl has developed such a good memory is connected to hunting over its territory. The owl's ability to remember the positions of every tree and branch in an area of woodland enables it to get around with the maximum efficiency and obtain as much prey as possible with the minimum of effort. It also explains how it can hunt in the dark of night – even though its vision is no better than a human's, it remembers exactly where the branches and other obstacles lie so it can avoid them. When owls are found with broken bones they are often young and inexperienced individuals that have not yet learned their way around.

Establishing a territory

Tawny owls pair for life, although some males have been known to pair with more than one female. Usually, pairs will be

Silent, deadly flight

The tawny owl ambushes its prey. Its main hunting strategy is to sit motionless on a perch, waiting for the right moment to pounce on a small, unsuspecting mammal below.

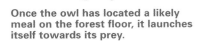

Once the owl has located a likely meal on the forest floor, it launches itself towards its prey.

seen together all year round – perhaps perched in the same tree. They remain in their territory throughout the year, often for many years in succession.

The breeding year starts in October or November, when established pairs confirm ownership of their territory. Young owls born earlier in the year will now be sexually mature and ready to breed. They must first lay claim to a territory – perhaps within that of their parents. This is crucial to their future success, because if they fail to gain a hunting ground, they are likely to starve.

Initially, boundary disputes are highly aggressive, accompanied by a great deal of hooting and calling. The male tawny owl establishes the territorial boundaries and the female selects the nest hole. Gradually, the pairs settle down and start to roost together. Towards the end of the year, the male starts to bring food to his mate. This 'courtship feeding', as it is called, not only confirms their partnership, but enables the female to build up reserves ready for breeding. During courtship the male will also chase the female round and round the territory, making screeching noises.

Nesting and breeding

The tawny owl's traditional nest site is a natural hollow in a tree, but they will also nest in chimneys, ruins, old nests made by other birds (especially crows, magpies and buzzards), and even in squirrels' dreys. In areas where few mature trees are found, such as in south-west Scotland, tawny owls also nest on the ground. One resourceful pair even set up home under the back seat of an old car abandoned on a rubbish tip.

The eggs, which are white and round, are laid early, in March, so that the parents can catch enough small mammals

◄ **Tawny owls like to nest in hollow trees, which is why they are often found in woodland or farmland where old trees are available. In young plantations, few natural hollows occur so the owls will use any substitutes provided, usually in the form of large, tunnel-like nestboxes.**

On silent wings, the owl drops swiftly down from above. The chosen prey has little warning of the owl's sudden approach.

▶ Voles and other small woodland mammals are the tawny owl's main prey. However, it often takes small rabbits, moles and earthworms, too, as well as many birds.

At the last moment the owl spreads its wings to slow its descent over its prey before extending its powerful talons.

for their chicks before the undergrowth grows and hides them. Usually, an interval of three to four days elapses between the laying of the first and second eggs, but occasionally this is as little as 48 hours. Two to four eggs will be laid in all, and these are incubated by the female alone. It seems that incubation doesn't start until the second egg is laid, and the first egg is not always the first to hatch.

After hatching, the male bird brings food for the young. The female does not leave the nest until the chicks are six to seven days old, after which she may take flight to make brief hunting trips of her own. Otherwise, she remains nearby. Young tawny owls depend on their parents for food for up to three months after leaving the nest, and it is at this time – while they are learning to fend for themselves – that there is a very high rate of mortality among the young owls.

Tawny owls are not only aggressive in defence of their territories but also when protecting their young. The female can be particularly dangerous, and mothers have been known to attack a person approaching the nest, even to the point of drawing blood with their talons. Two such incidents in Britain have resulted in the victim losing an eye. One of these was

MOBBING PARTIES

Sometimes parties of small birds discover a tawny owl in its daytime roost and attack it with much calling and commotion. Tits, robins, blackbirds, thrushes, jays and others are active in these 'mobbing' parties, all birds that the tawny may prey upon during its night-time forays. The small birds crowd closer and closer to the owl, flicking their wings as if daring it to respond.

The calls used by mobbing birds are special ones, understood by all species. These calls alert other birds in the neighbourhood to the presence of a predator and call on them to help drive it away. Blackbirds use a loud 'chink chink' call and jays may even seem to imitate the hoot of the owl, as if to identify the predator.

Sometimes the owl tries to fly away to escape its attackers, which follow it with even noisier alarm calls. But if, as usually happens, the owl remains motionless on its perch, the angry birds get tired and eventually leave it alone.

All species of owls are mobbed by songbirds, but in Britain the tawny owl is a particular focus of attacks. Small birds are alert to the general shape of the owl, even when it is hardly visible to the human eye. Over the centuries, hunters have used owl decoys to catch birds for the pot by smearing sticky bird lime on the twigs and branches around a tethered owl, so that when birds come in to mob it they are caught. Sadly, this practice still continues in some parts of the world.

Quite often, when a tawny owl is roosting during the day, small birds will mob it. The birds cannot harm the owl, which may just sit still until they give up.

Tawny owls leave the nest at about five weeks old, long before they are able to look after themselves. At first they remain in the vicinity and their parents return to feed them. The young make special calls to ensure the adults can find them, which prevent the brood from being mixed up with any other young tawny families in the area. Young owls depend on their parents for food for up to three months after they leave the nest, and during this time they gradually learn to fend for themselves and to establish territories of their own.

At this stage of their lives, owlets are often discovered by well-meaning people who think that the youngsters have lost their parents or been abandoned. The adults will almost certainly be close by and will return to care for them. It is best to leave them alone – hand-reared owls cannot be released into the wild because they haven't been taught how to hunt and would therefore starve.

The eggs are incubated by the female. She is very protective of her family and will attack anything considered to be a threat. An owl's sharp talons can inflict serious wounds.

In spite of their cuddly appearance, tawny owl chicks are quite fierce and will hiss and snap their beaks violently if they sense danger.

Eric Hosking, the famous bird photographer. Extreme aggression is unusual, though, and mostly occurs in areas frequented by humans.

Fluctuating numbers
During the 19th century, tawny numbers decreased significantly – a decline attributed to persecution by gamekeepers who thought that tawnies were affecting the availability of young rabbits and hares. From 1900 to 1930 numbers started to rise, especially after the decline in gamekeeping during the First World War. In some areas this increase continued until the early 1960s, apart from some minor fluctuations caused by severe winters and the use of organochlorine pesticides. Since then, tawny numbers have remained largely stable. Some declines in agricultural areas are probably linked with the loss of old elms and other trees that provide safe nest sites, and perhaps the use of agrochemicals.

Compared with the barn owl, the tawny owl is a versatile bird. Its repertoire of hunting techniques enables it to catch different types of prey, so it is not affected by the scarcity of one particular species. Also, unlike the barn owl, tawnies build up their fat reserves before the onset of winter. Not only does this aid the owl's chances of survival, but it also leaves the female in better condition at the start of the breeding season.

The tawny owl has not only maintained, but also extended, the areas in which it lives. It has spread through gardens in suburbs and parks in the centre of towns and cities. Its readiness to accept nestboxes has enabled it to move into new environments, such as mature conifer plantations, which are now found in several parts of the country. The number of potential territories is the limiting factor for population growth, but for now the future of the tawny owl in Britain looks secure.

WILDLIFE WATCH

Where can I see tawny owls?

● Tawny owls are noisy birds, especially in the winter months. Their calls will indicate where to look for them at dusk, but there is no substitute for patiently waiting until one comes into sight. During the day, the owl's position is most likely to be given away by the alarm calls of small birds when it is being mobbed. It is always worth investigating to find out what is going on, and you may be lucky enough to see the owl.

● In urban areas, tawny owls are often easier to see than in the countryside. This is because they have fewer places to hide and also because the city night is never really dark. Street lamps provide sufficient light for you to spot the owls, even late at night. Often they sit on television aerials or chimneys, right out in the open.

◄ **Both parents care for the young. The male works overtime to catch additional food for his family while the female remains close to her chicks, especially for the first few days after hatching.**

▲ **The young can fly when they are about five weeks old. At this stage, they still retain much of their fluffy down. This is gradually replaced by normal feathers, often more greyish than in the adult.**

Recognising thrushes

Several species of thrush are found in Britain, from the familiar blackbird to the scarcer ring ouzel. Their attractive plumage and melodious song brighten even the dullest winter's day.

The mistle thrush is a dauntless songster and continues to sing come rain or shine. Its loud, fluting song is delivered from the topmost branches of trees.

Most gardens and areas of woodland in Britain are home to at least one species of thrush. Familiar garden thrushes include the blackbird and song thrush. Others are easy to see at the right time of year and in the correct locations, but are more specialised in their habits.

All of Britain's six regularly occurring thrush species have a similar body shape and medium-length pointed bills. These are ideally suited to probing the ground and extracting earthworms. Indeed, all of them consume these invertebrates with relish.

Feeding strategies

Blackbirds adopt a more vigorous approach to feeding than some of their cousins, and typically flick over debris such as leaf litter in the hope of finding a worm or a spider hidden underneath. However, the prize for creativity must go to the song thrush, which specialises in feeding on snails, holding the lip of the shell while smashing it against a stone or any other hard object that will serve as an anvil.

Berries and fruit are staple elements in the diet of most thrushes, but being seasonal

Bold and resourceful, the blackbird has successfully adapted to living near human habitation. When snow blankets the ground, the blackbird turns its attention to berries and other fruits, often attracted to gardens in search of this food.

and unpredictable in quantity they tend to be feasted upon in an opportunistic manner. The mistle thrush, by contrast, has a more systematic approach. Established pairs or single birds will often make an isolated holly, hawthorn or other berry-bearing shrub or tree the centre of their winter territory and guard this larder jealously against all intruders. They also feed on mistletoe berries, hence their name.

Beautiful voices

Many members of the thrush family are renowned songsters, and the blackbird's beautiful, rich, varied fluty medley is a notable element in the dawn chorus of most British gardens. Song thrushes also sing their hearts out in mature gardens and woodlands, while mistle thrushes are typically associated with open woodland in rural districts and increasingly in urban parks. The simple song of the ring ouzel is heard only by those venturing to its upland haunts.

Migratory habits

The song of the fieldfare and redwing, which is used to attract mates in spring, is seldom heard in Britain. These are winter visitors and just a few pairs remain to breed. The ring ouzel is a summer migrant breeder. For the blackbird, song and mistle thrush, however, the situation is more complicated.

In the winter, the alarm calls of fieldfares and redwings are as familiar to birdwatchers as the blackbird's calls are to gardeners.

Although all three species can be seen in Britain all year round, it is not necessarily the same birds that are involved in all sightings. British birds are migratory to a greater or lesser degree, depending on the area in which they breed. In winter, there are also influxes from mainland Europe.

▲ Shortly after their arrival in autumn, migrant redwings often congregate on berry-bearing bushes, which they strip of fruit in just a few days.

▶ As with other juvenile thrushes, young song thrushes have spotted plumage. This enables them to remain concealed from predatory eyes.

EASY GUIDE TO SPOTTING THRUSHES

Blackbird

Ring ouzel

Song thrush

Mistle thrush

Fieldfare

Redwing

WHAT ARE THRUSHES?

● Thrushes are plump-bodied birds with short necks. They belong to the family Turdidae, along with the smaller chats (such as the robin and nightingale). All six thrush species regularly seen in Britain are in the genus *Turdus*.

● Five of the six species of thrush that can be found in Britain are birds of parks, woodland and farmland. However, the sixth species, the ring ouzel, is restricted as a breeder to the upland regions of Britain.

Distribution map key

☐ Not present	☐ Present during winter months
◼ Present all year round	☐ Present during summer months

HOW CAN I IDENTIFY THRUSHES?

● An all-black bird with a yellow bill and eye ring is certain to be a male blackbird. Females have brown plumage.

● The ring ouzel resembles the male blackbird, but has a white crescent on its breast (duller in females). Males are blackish, while females have dark brown scaly-looking plumage.

● In the fieldfare, redwing, song and mistle thrushes, the sexes look similar.

● Song and mistle thrushes are similar in appearance, but the former is smaller and has buffish orange rather than white underwings. The two birds also differ in flight style.

● The fieldfare has a chestnut back and greyish head and rump. Its tail is black and it has spotted underparts.

● Redwings have reddish underwings and flanks and striking striped facial markings.

BLACKBIRD *Turdus merula*

The male blackbird is easy to recognise – a combination of glossy black plumage, yellow eye ring and golden yellow bill are unique features. The female is dark brown with a variable rufous tinge to her dark-spotted underside. Her eye ring is dark brown and her bill is never as bright as the male's. Juveniles are similar to females, but more spotted.

● SIZE
24–25cm (9½–10in) long

● NEST
Robust cup of grass and leaves lined with mud mixed with grass, in fork of branch

● BREEDING
Lays 4–5 light blue, speckled eggs in March–May

● FOOD
Insects, earthworms, fruits and seeds

● HABITAT
Wide range of wooded habitats, including parks and gardens

● VOICE
Sharp, ringing *'chook-chook-chook'* alarm calls and rich, fluty song

● DISTRIBUTION
Very common throughout Britain and Ireland

The blackbird is recognisable, even at a distance, simply by the way it moves and especially by the way it raises its tail on landing. In winter, numbers are swelled by migrants.

Brownish plumage and brownish or yellowish bill

Female

Variably mottled underparts

Yellow bill and eye ring

Jet black plumage

Dark legs

Male

RING OUZEL *Turdus torquatus*

The ring ouzel is secretive and easily alarmed. The male has black plumage (which appears partly scaly due to pale feather edges), a black head and a bold white, crescent-shaped bib. The yellow bill has a black tip. The female is browner than the male and appears more scaly. Her bib is duller. Juveniles resemble females, but have indistinct bibs.

● SIZE
23–24cm (9–9½in) long

● NEST
Cup of grass and leaves, in crevice among boulders

● BREEDING
Lays 4–5 blue-green, speckled eggs in April–May

● FOOD
Mostly invertebrates, some seeds and berries in autumn

● HABITAT
Moors and mountains

● VOICE
Chattering alarm calls and song of a few fluty notes

● DISTRIBUTION
A summer visitor to northern and western Britain and parts of western Ireland

The ring ouzel was once known as the 'mountain blackbird' due to its preference for upland regions. A shy, wary bird, it is best looked for on rocky crags.

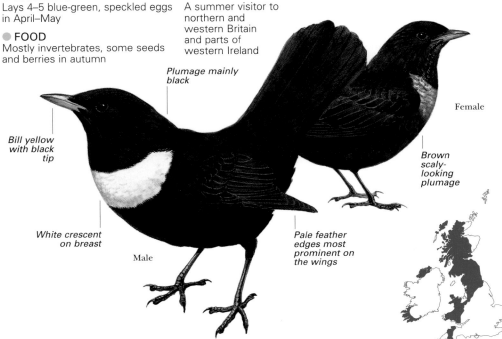

Plumage mainly black

Female

Bill yellow with black tip

White crescent on breast

Male

Brown scaly-looking plumage

Pale feather edges most prominent on the wings

SONG THRUSH *Turdus philomelos*

A strongly patterned breast and pale facial markings identify the song thrush. The underparts are white with a golden brown wash on the sides of the breast and on the flanks. The breast is densely marked with blackish brown spots that fade out on the belly. Juveniles have pale streaks and speckles on their backs.

● **SIZE**
23cm (9in) long

● **NEST**
Grassy cup lined with smooth mud, in trees, shrubs, on banks, ledges or ground among thick vegetation

● **BREEDING**
Lays 3–5 bright blue eggs with blackish spots in April–May

● **FOOD**
Invertebrates, including snails; fruits and berries in winter

● **HABITAT**
Mixed woodlands, parks, gardens and hedgerows

● **VOICE**
Various short alarm notes, including *'tchik tchik tchik'*, a softer *'tsip'* flight call, and a rich, repetitive musical song

● **DISTRIBUTION**
Common across Britain and Ireland

The song thrush is often seen in gardens and parks, singing joyfully from a high perch or racing across the lawn in search of snails.

Rich brown upperparts

Indistinct facial markings

Spots are arrowhead shaped

Golden buff wash on flanks

MISTLE THRUSH *Turdus viscivorus*

Another thrush with a distinctively patterned breast, the mistle thrush is the largest member of the family. Its upperparts are greyer and paler than the song thrush's, and it has paler, greyer cheeks and neck and a longer tail. In flight, its white underwings may be seen. Juveniles resemble adults, but have white-spotted heads, backs and wing coverts.

● **SIZE**
27cm (10¾in) long

● **NEST**
Large cup of grass, roots and leaves mixed with mud, lined with finer grasses, in high tree fork

● **BREEDING**
Lays 3–5 pale bluish eggs with darker blotches in late February–May

● **FOOD**
Invertebrates; also berries and fruits in autumn and winter

● **HABITAT**
Open woodlands, parks, gardens, orchards and hedgerows

● **VOICE**
Harsh, rattling alarm calls, short, loud, simple fluty song from high perch; sings in stormy weather

● **DISTRIBUTION**
Common across Britain and Ireland

The mistle thrush has a pot-bellied appearance and an erect stance. It may be seen hunting for worms on playing fields, provided the area has some trees nearby.

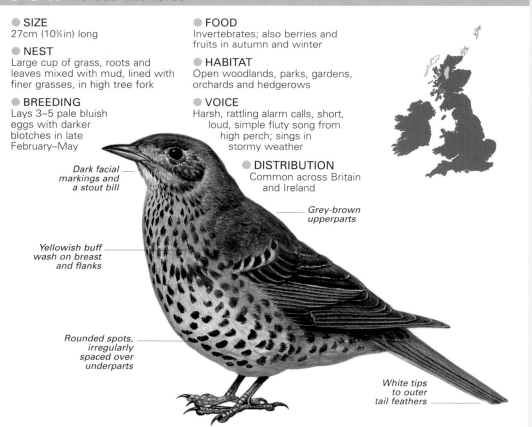

Dark facial markings and a stout bill

Grey-brown upperparts

Yellowish buff wash on breast and flanks

Rounded spots, irregularly spaced over underparts

White tips to outer tail feathers

FIELDFARE *Turdus pilaris*

The fieldfare has a slate grey head, nape and rump and a chestnut back. The flight feathers and the tip of the tail are black and the underparts are golden-orange with bold black arrowhead-shaped markings. The bill is at least partly yellow. Juveniles lack the adult's strong colours and look more like mistle thrushes.

● SIZE
25.5cm (10¼in) long

● NEST
Bulky nest of twigs and roots, lined with mud and grass, in tree or on the ground

● BREEDING
Lays 5–6 light blue eggs with reddish speckles in April–May

● FOOD
Insects and worms; fruits and seeds in winter

● HABITAT
Open woodland, gardens, parks and open farmland

● VOICE
Chattering contact notes and a weak, warbling song (rarely heard)

● DISTRIBUTION
A common winter visitor from northern and eastern Europe and Russia; rare breeding bird in northern Britain

Grey head and mainly yellow bill

Chestnut back

Black flight feathers

Rich golden flush to breast

Dark tail contrasts with grey rump

From October, when large flocks of migrant fieldfares arrive in Britain, these thrushes can be seen in open fields and parks. Most of them remain until about April.

REDWING *Turdus iliacus*

Britain's smallest species of thrush, the redwing, is easy to recognise due to its extensive red flanks and underwings. The upperparts are dark brown and the head has creamy stripes above the eye and below the cheeks. The underparts are yellowish brown with dark streaks and fade to off-white. Juveniles resemble adults but their backs have buff spots.

● SIZE
21cm (8¼in) long

● NEST
Cup of grasses, twigs and moss, lined with mud and grass, high in a tree

● BREEDING
Lays 4–6 pale blue or greenish, red-brown speckled eggs in May–June

● FOOD
Mainly insects and other invertebrates; fruits and berries in winter

● HABITAT
Breeds in open woodlands, scrub and birch thickets; prefers open grassland in winter

● VOICE
Jumbled, fluty song and '*seee-ip*' flight call (longer, hoarser than similar call of song thrush)

● DISTRIBUTION
A common winter visitor from Iceland, northern Europe and Russia; small numbers breed in Scotland

Blackish brown bill with yellowish base

Chocolate brown upperparts

Short, brown tail

Underparts spotted with red flanks

Migrant redwings arrive in Britain from September to November. They form roving flocks that visit gardens and other areas with short grass in search of invertebrates.

The green woodpecker

A loud, laughing call heralds the arrival of a green woodpecker. Although shy and elusive, this bird may sometimes be seen hopping awkwardly across the grass in search of ants, its favourite food.

A yellow-tinged, creamy coloured neck, red crown and black face make the green woodpecker a most striking bird. Males are distinguished from females by the red centre to the black lower cheek stripe.

With its green back, red crown and bright yellow rump, the green woodpecker is an easy bird to recognise. It is the largest woodpecker in Britain, and very different in appearance from its two smaller black-and-white cousins, the great and lesser spotted woodpeckers.

While the green woodpecker does perform the usual repertoire of woodpecker-like behaviour – drilling into wood with its strong, chisel-shaped bill and hanging tenaciously on to the vertical surface of tree trunks – it is equally at home on the ground. It hops about with a distinctive upright posture and uses its long, sticky tongue to scoop up ants from ant hills. It rarely drums on trees and when it does so, the roll is feebler than

that of the other two British woodpeckers. Much more characteristic is its laughing, ringing call, which is audible at several hundred metres, and is often the first indication that one of these attractive birds is in the area.

While most woodpeckers are found in forests, or somewhere with an abundance of trees, this is not the case with the green woodpecker. Over the course of evolution, the species switched from a mainly arboreal diet to one that involves hunting for ants on the ground.

THE YAFFLE

The popularity of the green woodpecker is reflected in its large number of local names – the 'English parrot' is one, but the most widespread is 'yaffle'. This has a long history and derives from the bird's attractive, loud laughing call (a repeated *'peeu-peeu-peeu'* sound).

Despite being readily identifiable, the yaffle's call is quite variable. It may be loud and long – with up to 20 individual notes – or much shorter and quite soft. The loud calls are clearly intended to advertise the bird's presence, both for territorial defence and also, in spring, to attract a mate. The quieter notes are generally used by the bird as contact calls to keep in touch with its mate or fledged chicks.

Another common name is 'rain bird'. This probably derives from ancient Mediterranean beliefs that endowed the bird with the gift of prophecy including foretelling rain.

GREEN WOODPECKER FACT FILE

Parks, meadows and woods are favoured by the green woodpecker, the largest of the three species found in Britain. Its pointed head and tail and brilliant yellow rump mark it out as it glides gently down to the ground, where it spends much of its time.

● NAME
Common names: green woodpecker, yaffle, English parrot, rain bird
Scientific name: *Picus viridis*

● HABITAT
Parks, gardens, farmland, open woodland with grassy areas

● DISTRIBUTION
Most common south of line from mid-Wales to the Wash; in Scottish lowlands north to Inverness; rare in uplands, absent from Isle of Man and Ireland

● STATUS
Roughly 15,000 pairs

● SIZE
Length 30–33cm (12–13in); weight 180–220g (6–8oz)

● KEY FEATURES
A powerful bird, larger and bulkier than the great spotted woodpecker; back and wings dull green, rump bright yellow, main wing and tail feathers blackish brown; long red cap from forehead to nape, big black cheek stripes (with red centre in males); sides of head, neck and underparts yellowish cream, spotted in juveniles; bill long, sharp, powerful

● HABITS
Prefers to hunt on ground, especially in grass; raids ants' nests; sometimes drums on wood to advertise presence, but drums quietly and only in spring

● VOICE
Classic 'yaffle' call – a loud, clear, ringing 'peeu-peeu-peeu…', comprising 3–20 notes, given in many different circumstances

● FOOD
Ants of various species, including adults, pupae, larvae and eggs, taken throughout year; also beetles and flies and their larvae and caterpillars taken by hacking into tree trunks or branches

● BREEDING
First eggs laid early April; late broods and replacements started as late as June

● NEST
Hole excavated in tree, mainly by male, 40–50cm (16–20in) deep, bigger than that of other species; entrance round or oval, 6–7cm (2½–2¾in) in diameter, sited 1–5m (3–16ft) above ground; no lining material brought in from outside and eggs laid on sparse layer of wood chips resulting from the excavation

● EGGS
Clutch of 5–7 white, smooth and glossy eggs; 17–19 day incubation by both sexes

● YOUNG
Naked chicks brooded for first few days, both sexes feed young in nest; fledge by about 3 weeks, cared for by parents for further 3–7 weeks; one brood per season

Distribution map key

■ Present all year round

□ Not present

The juvenile lacks the definite facial markings of the adult and is instead heavily streaked on the neck and breast. Its green back is dotted with pale spots.

The strong, chisel-like bill is used for probing the ground for food and excavating the nest hole.

The adult has a distinct red cap.

Powerful feet, with long toes usually 2 pointing forward, 2 pointing back, and strong talons are used for gripping tree bark.

Stiff tail feathers are used as a prop to stabilise the bird as it climbs.

The green woodpecker has retained the basic woodpecker tool-kit because, despite its largely terrestrial feeding habits, it still nests in tree holes. Like other woodpeckers, it has a sharp beak to excavate soft wood and 'zygodactyl' feet – two toes pointing forward and two back. Along with the specially stiffened tail feathers, these remarkable toes help the bird to cling to tree trunks.

◄ The remarkably long, flexible tongue of the green woodpecker is used to probe into crevices in tree trunks, searching for the larvae of wood-boring insects. The tongue's sticky tip captures the grubs easily.

The choice of nesting tree is important. The trunk must have quite a wide diameter for the birds to build a nest in it. Ideal trees are those that are located close to suitable hunting grounds, such as on the edge of a wood, in an isolated copse or even a mature tree standing alone in grassland. Mature parkland or wood pasture with plenty of permanent grassland kept short, almost manicured, by livestock or wild animals will attract green woodpeckers. The open, springy turf of downland in south-western England is excellent for ants, and trees nearby are likely to be inhabited by green woodpeckers.

Areas of heathland also provide the combination of trees and ants that green woodpeckers like, but these valuable places are disappearing. Today the most densely populated green woodpecker habitats include the New Forest, the downland of southern England and the Breckland of East Anglia.

Hunting for ants

Finding ants' nests that can be safely raided is key to the survival of green woodpeckers. Short grass is crucial, because it allows the birds to locate the

The green woodpecker has a distinctly undulating flight. Its broad, round-tipped wings help negotiate take off and landing on a vertical tree trunk.

Lucky dip

A green woodpecker pokes its pointed bill into an ant hill and then extends its long, sticky tongue to probe the holes and passages for ants, eggs, larvae and pupae.

The green woodpecker's tongue has a very mobile tip, which is ideal for reaching around corners.

The strict order inside an ant hill breaks down as the inhabitants rush about in a vain attempt to move their eggs to safety and repair damage to the nest.

GREEN WOODPECKER CALENDAR

JANUARY ● FEBRUARY

Food is less readily available in winter, but ant hills may be found and attacked even under a blanket of snow. Other food may also be taken – including larvae inside rotten wood.

MARCH ● APRIL

Occasional drumming resumes as males establish territories and the birds spend a lot of time calling and excavating their nest holes. Egg laying takes place from early April until mid-June.

MAY ● JUNE

The young hatch and demand a constant supply of food. Both parents carry thousands of ants back to the nest, regurgitating them from the stomach to feed each chick.

JULY ● AUGUST

By the beginning of July, the young of many nests will have fledged, but they are still looked after by their parents for several weeks. Generally, each adult cares for half the brood.

SEPTEMBER ● OCTOBER

Young birds move a short distance to find places of their own to live. They will now live mostly solitary lives until ready to breed, while the older birds may remain closer together.

NOVEMBER ● DECEMBER

By now, the birds have got to know their local area well, knowledge that will be vital in the coming weeks as the weather becomes colder and the hours of daylight for hunting get shorter.

nests while keeping a look-out for any predators, such as cats, foxes, stoats or sparrowhawks, that could be approaching them as they feed. Short grass also enables the heat of the sun to warm the ground, improving the conditions for the ants.

In the 1950s, the loss of rabbits to myxomatosis was a setback for green woodpeckers. The grass grew long without being constantly nibbled by rabbits, and the ants suffered as a result. Consequently, the decline in ants caused the green woodpecker population to crash.

When a woodpecker locates an ants' nest, it will often spend many minutes – even an hour – feeding at a single spot. By attacking the nest, the bird aggravates the ants, which rush to the surface to repel the intruder. The green woodpecker is not immune to the chemical weapons deployed by many ants, nor to the sharp jaws of the large-headed worker caste of the bigger species. A bird may be seen

stamping its feet and shaking its head as the insects penetrate its defences. It may even be forced to fly off to clean up.

Having evolved to feed on ants, the green woodpecker's bill is not as strong as that of its cousins, and it has to restrict its arboreal feeding attempts to trees that are soft and rotten. However, the bill is strong enough to enable the bird to excavate earth. In winter, it may have to dig through snow up to 30cm (12in)

deep in order to reach an ants' nest. If the snow has a frozen crust, this is no mean feat.

The most important tool that the green woodpecker possesses for feeding on ants is its tongue. This is remarkably long, extending an extraordinary 10cm (4in) from the tip of the bill, and is a precision instrument capable of very delicate movement. When not in use, the tongue is retracted and

Open areas of close-cropped vegetation are the ideal hunting grounds for green woodpeckers. For this reason, they may sometimes be spotted hopping around on garden lawns, probing for ants in the soil.

WOODPECKER VANDALS

The green woodpecker is a shy bird that rarely comes into contact with humans. However, there have been instances of the birds apparently attacking beehives. They do not always seem to be in search of a meal and it is thought that they are attracted by the buzzing of the insects.

Several records exist of woodpeckers launching attacks on the shingles of church spires. These thin wooden 'slates' – usually made of cedar – overlap down the spire and are much too thin to have insects living in them. However, the wind can make them hum and it is almost certainly this noise that attracts the birds. With their powerful bills they are capable of inflicting hundreds of pounds worth of damage in a very short time.

Surprisingly, green woodpeckers have been known to cause damage to hives. While they may be in search of bees and their grubs, it is more likely that they are merely attracted by the noise.

The young fledge in around three weeks but continue to be fed by their parents for up to seven more weeks. Eventually, when ignored by the adults, they are forced to forage for themselves and move to new areas.

coiled up around the skull, supported by a special long, curving bone. The muscle that controls the tongue is as big as the bird's brain.

The bird's well-developed salivary glands produce a sticky covering over the tongue, which enables the green woodpecker to capture ants easily. The other British woodpeckers have clusters of barbs at the tips of their tongues, which enable them to spear large larvae hidden deep in tunnels in tree trunks. The green woodpecker's tongue has far fewer barbs, arranged in rows, and a wide, flattened tip that is ideal for using as a sticky lasso to scoop up ants. Many ants are simply

◄ **When feeding young, adult birds return to the nest site with their throat pouches crammed full of insect grubs. The chicks consume as many as the parents can find. Ant larvae are a favourite.**

picked from the surface but, once the green woodpecker has probed a nest with its bill, it will use its tongue to explore the galleries and extract the ants from within.

The number of ants available to the woodpeckers in an average territory is enormous. This is just as well, since a thousand or more may be eaten in one sitting. During a detailed study of one green woodpecker nest with seven young, it was recorded that each chick received approximately 800g (28oz) of food before fledging. It was calculated that this single brood consumed around 1.5 million ants and pupae. These will have been swallowed by the adults (both the male and female share the task of feeding their young) and then regurgitated as a milky paste that the swiftly growing chicks can easily digest.

Social behaviour

Green woodpeckers are usually solitary, and will be seen in pairs only during the breeding season in spring. In late summer and early autumn, parent birds are normally each accompanied by two or three youngsters. Yet for six months of the year it is unusual to see two birds

◄ **A green woodpecker is normally quick to retreat at the slightest disturbance. If intent on feeding, however, it may temporarily 'freeze' until the danger has passed, when the bird may resume its hunt for insect grubs.**

▲ Feather care is as important to green woodpeckers as it is to other birds. An individual may have a favourite woodland pool to which it returns time after time.

▶ During the summer, the green woodpecker does not have to raid an ant hill to get a meal – lines of foraging ants can simply be picked off the heather as they march past.

together. This does not mean that each woodpecker lives in isolation. The roost site, which may be used for several years, is often shared by paired birds even though they are seldom seen together during the day. Every individual is fully aware of its neighbours – their calls can be heard at long range, enabling each bird to recognise other woodpeckers and discern their location. This communication allows green woodpeckers to know where they stand in the social network.

During the breeding season the birds exhibit some interesting behaviour. Like the great spotted woodpecker, the green woodpecker has an elaborate courtship

display, whereby the male makes spiral pursuits of a female around a tree trunk. When a male green woodpecker meets a rival male, both birds begin swaying their heads from side to side with wings spread, tails fanned and crests raised.

Each green woodpecker has a home range of up to 250 hectares (620 acres), but not all of this terrain is necessarily the domain of a single bird. Green woodpeckers do not move far and territories are often separated by areas without any birds at all. However, in places with plenty of suitable habitat and food, the boost given to the local woodpecker population may mean that pairs are forced to live closer

together in territories as small as 10 hectares (25 acres). These may not be defended right up to the boundaries, but the environs of the nest hole will be exclusively 'owned' by a single bird. Drumming, which is not at all common, is concentrated on the nest site. Both sexes drum and the best time to hear it is in the early morning from March to May.

Even with a large brood, each parent usually collects enough ants to feed each of its demanding offspring at each visit – a task that can take several minutes.

WILDLIFE WATCH

Where can I see green woodpeckers?

● Open woodland and parkland with large populations of ants are good places to watch for green woodpeckers. Areas of farmland with isolated woods and permanent pasture are favoured, too, as is open heathland. Green woodpeckers may frequent large gardens in rural settings.

● They need trees in which to nest, but areas of dense, unbroken woodland are not suitable. Open, grassy areas where the birds can find ants are more important.

● Look for a medium-sized bird with a very pronounced, 'bounding' flight profile. The rather dull, greyish olive colour of the upperparts contrasts with the bright yellow of the rump.

● A pleasant, liquid laughing call indicates that a green woodpecker is about. It can be heard over a long distance and may be answered by other birds within earshot. Stay quiet in case the calling bird is on the move. After a few minutes you will have a reasonable idea of how many birds there are in the vicinity.

● After the young have fledged, each adult will have two, occasionally three, youngsters in tow. They will often spend extended periods of time in areas where there are plentiful food supplies.

● One telltale sign of a green woodpecker's presence is its droppings, which are full of the remains of ants and resemble cigarette ash.

The jay

The most colourful member of the crow family, the jay has a buff body and electric-blue wing patches that often stand out against the drab winter landscape – and it flashes a white rump when it flies away.

Jays are quite common throughout Britain, but it is often difficult to get a good view of one since they are very shy. In the winter, jays can be seen digging around in the soil and among fallen leaves, where they may have buried some acorns or beech nuts in the autumn. Although jays eat many other types of food, including insects, eggs, nestlings, small mammals and seeds, the buried larder of food is crucial in the winter and enables the birds to survive when other food is hard to find.

The first sign of jays is usually their raucous, grating alarm call issuing from the undergrowth of a wood or copse as the birds move about in the shelter of the vegetation. If a bird emerges into a woodland clearing, or flits through the canopy, it is instantly recognisable by its bright white rump patch and flash of blue on the wings.

Jays are a little larger than a jackdaw or town pigeon. They have broad wings and a characteristically unsteady or undulating flight. On the ground they tend to jump or bound along, rather than walk or run. In many ways they are contradictory birds – colourful yet often surprisingly hard to spot; bold and aggressive at times, yet frequently shy and skulking; harmful to other songbirds yet beneficial to oak trees in spreading their seeds; beautiful to look at but with harsh, grating calls. They are intelligent, too. In common with other members of the crow family, they adapt quickly to changes in food supply, and remember where they have hidden caches of food.

Geographical spread

Jays are common throughout Europe, except for the far north, and are found right across Asia to Japan and China, as well as in North Africa. There are several subspecies, each occupying a different area, and each with slightly different colours and patterns of plumage. The British subspecies is also found in Belgium and the Netherlands, but different subspecies occur in Ireland and other parts of Europe, North Africa and Asia.

An estimated 160,000 pairs live in Britain, with a further 10,000 or so in Ireland. During the 19th and 20th centuries up to the Second World War (and to a lesser degree up to the 1960s), jays and magpies were ruthlessly persecuted by gamekeepers because they were perceived to be major predators of young gamebirds. This resulted in a decrease in numbers in woodland and farmland. However, with the decline in gamekeeping over the past 50 years or so, the threat has lessened and jay numbers have recovered. Another reason for the recovery may be the spread of conifer plantations, which offer new breeding sites for the birds.

In Britain, jays are most abundant in the south, notably in Kent, Sussex, Surrey and Hampshire, although they are found as far north as central Scotland and seem to be slowly extending their range even farther northwards. However, they are still rare north and west of the Great Glen.

In winter, the jay searches for berries with which to supplement its diet. Like crows, it has innovative feeding habits and quickly finds new items to eat when its favourite foods are scarce.

JAY FACT FILE

Unlike most other members of the crow family, jays are bright, colourful birds with bold black-and-white wing bars. Males and females are similar in appearance and are indistinguishable in the field.

● **NAMES**
Common name: jay
Latin name: *Garrulus glandarius*

● **HABITAT**
Woodland (especially with oaks), plantations, copses, hedgerows

● **DISTRIBUTION**
Most numerous in south and east of Britain but found throughout most of British Isles, except far north and west

● **STATUS**
Around 170,000 pairs in the British Isles

● **SIZE**
Length 34cm (13½in); similar to a jackdaw but much paler and more colourful

● **KEY FEATURES**
Shows white rump-patch in flight; patch of electric-blue feathers on wings

● **HABITS**
Secretive, and more likely to be heard than seen; territorial and in pairs or family groups during breeding season, but spring flocks may include up to 30 birds

● **VOICE**
Often makes raucous, rasping *'skaaak'* call of alarm as well as a variety of other calls, including mewing sounds and mimicry of many other birds; rarely heard song is a medley of quiet bubbling, gurgling or clicking sounds

● **FOOD**
Earthworms, beetles, small mammals and eggs and nestlings of other birds, as well as many types of fruit and seeds, including beech mast and acorns

● **BREEDING**
Eggs laid in April or May; single brood

● **NEST**
Made from sticks, often set low down in a bush or tree

● **EGGS**
5–7 (occasionally more), pale greenish blue with very fine brown speckles; incubated for 16–17 days, by female only

● **YOUNG**
Naked at first; fledge in about 21–22 days but fed by parents for a further 3–5 weeks

▲ **Young birds lie still and quiet in the nest, but stretch upwards and open their beaks when a parent returns. The bright pink gape of their beaks elicits a feeding response from the adult.**

Distribution map key

  Present all year round

Not present

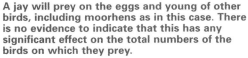

A jay will prey on the eggs and young of other birds, including moorhens as in this case. There is no evidence to indicate that this has any significant effect on the total numbers of the birds on which they prey.

A striking feature is the crest of black and white feathers on the top of the head, raised in display or when the bird is excited.

The jay has a bright pink-buff plumage, surprisingly hard to see in foliage but conspicuous when out in the open.

A distinctive patch of electric blue feathers can be seen on the primary coverts below the bend of the wing.

JAY CALENDAR

JANUARY ● FEBRUARY

The jay relies upon its food caches to see it through the cold weather, retrieving stored nuts from beneath the snow. The birds are at risk from sharp-eyed sparrowhawks, because their bright plumage stands out against muted winter colours.

MARCH ● APRIL

As spring approaches, jays gather in groups of varying sizes and begin displaying. Eventually the groups disperse as the birds pair up and start to defend their own breeding territories and build their nests.

MAY ● JUNE

Laid at the end of April and in early May, the eggs are incubated solely by the female, who is fed on the nest by her mate. After 16–17 days the naked young chicks hatch out and they consume large quantities of nutritious caterpillars brought to them by both their parents.

JULY ● AUGUST

By now the young have fledged and left the nest. They can often be seen following their parents, learning how to find food for themselves. Young jays resemble their parents closely, differing mainly in their somewhat duller plumage and shorter tail.

SEPTEMBER ● OCTOBER

This is the peak period for laying down stores of food for the coming winter. Jays can be seen systematically searching through beech and oak trees, gathering beech mast and acorns and hiding them in crevices, or burying them in the soil.

NOVEMBER ● DECEMBER

At this time of year, jay numbers are sometimes swelled by immigrants flying in from the Continent, especially if the nut crop has been poor there. If the weather is harsh, jays may visit bird tables for scraps of food.

In Ireland, there is evidence of a general decline, except in pockets in the west. They are common in woodland but less widespread overall since Ireland is much less wooded than Britain. For the same reason, jays are absent from most of the Fens.

Woodland home

Jays are essentially birds of temperate woodland – most notably deciduous broad-leaved woodland – especially where plenty of oak trees offer both shelter and acorns, a favourite food. In coniferous plantations, they usually breed at lower densities than in deciduous woods. In central and northern Europe, jays seem to prefer thickets of spruce or fir, perhaps because they offer a good refuge from attacks by sparrowhawks, the larger goshawks and other birds of prey.

Jays are increasingly found in parks and larger suburban gardens, and can often be spotted in cities, as long as there are green spaces and trees nearby. In quite a few places, jays are occasional, but wary, visitors to bird tables, especially in hard weather and in gardens that back on to woodland. Unlike other members of the crow family – the carrion crow, hooded crow, rook, raven, jackdaw, chough and magpie – jays are seldom seen foraging in fields or on hillsides. They tend to avoid more open country, such as pasture and farmland, and stick close to spinneys or copses. When acorns and beech mast are scarce, jays may move out of woodland in search of winter food supplies. In some years, following hard weather, many migrants end up in Britain from northern Europe.

Noisy gatherings

For most of the year, jays do not defend particular territories, but roam at random. In spring, they begin to gather together in groups, varying in size from just a few birds to 20 or 30. These larger groups may be noisy as individuals compete with each other and display to potential mates. Such gatherings are sometimes called jay 'marriages', and they involve chases and much calling. The song of the jay is rarely heard – it consists of a rather musical jumble of notes, but is soft and weak and does not carry very far. Much more commonly heard are their hoarse, rasping alarm calls. Jays sometimes make a plaintive mewing sound, very like the flight call of a buzzard. Eventually, the birds pair up and look for a nest site, which they defend against intruders.

Nesting and breeding

Jays like to nest where there is plenty of cover. The most favoured breeding sites are close to the edges of woods, near to woodland clearings, or in isolated copses. A typical site is woodland with dense undergrowth, including hazel shrubs, creepers and climbers, such as ivy and honeysuckle, or perhaps a thicket of closely spaced young trees and bushes.

From September to November, the jay searches through oak trees for acorns and forages for them on the ground below.

The bird can open its bill wide to swallow each acorn quickly.

Winter's secret store

One of the jay's survival strategies is to collect acorns and hoard them as emergency food supplies. Typical hiding places are under roots, moss or leaves, in the soil, or inside a log. A single jay can store thousands of acorns in its larders.

Both sexes help to construct the nest, which is a woven mass of twigs, with a small cup at its centre, lined with thinner twigs or with fine, flexible roots and mammal hair. It may be built within a couple of metres of the ground, often sited at a fork in a branch or where a branch joins the main trunk. If the tree supports ivy or honeysuckle, the nest may be built within this for extra concealment.

Jays have a single brood each year. The usual clutch is five to seven eggs, but may be as many as 10. The eggs, laid in April or May, are incubated solely by the female, and the young hatch after about 16 or 17 days. Jay nestlings are naked and helpless at first, but voraciously hungry. The parents work hard to feed them until they are large enough to leave the nest at about three weeks old. By then, the fledglings have their full plumage but they stay close to their parents for around another month.

Easy targets

Jays are long-lived birds and can potentially reach an age of 15 or 16 years, although few if any survive for this long in the wild. In hard winters, especially if the previous autumn's nut crop was poor, many die from starvation and cold.

Jays also have a number of natural predators. Weaker birds are sometimes taken by foxes but the major threat comes from the air, and specifically from sparrowhawks and the larger goshawks. The ponderous flight of a jay makes it easy for these swift woodland hawks to catch. Adult jays are usually too big for male sparrowhawks, but females are quite capable of catching them. Both sexes of goshawk can easily handle jays. In some parts of Europe jays are their favoured prey, but goshawks are rare in Britain.

Each bird can carry three or four acorns at a time, holding them temporarily in its throat pouch.

The distribution of several species of oak rely on the jay's habit of burying acorns. Unlike squirrels, jays do not nibble out the growing tip of the nut, so the acorn is able to germinate and grow into a tree.

'ANTING'

One of the jay's stranger habits is known as 'anting'. The bird stands on an ant hill, stirring it up so that the ants become angry. It spreads out its feathers so that the ants swarm all over its body and among its plumage. The insecticidal properties of the ants' defensive sprays of formic acid help the jay to rid itself of parasites. After a few minutes the jay flies off and works the secretions through its feathers by preening.

WILDLIFE WATCH

Where can I see jays?

● Look for jays in wooded areas, especially among oak trees. In autumn they make frequent trips to search for acorns. In winter, their plumage stands out as they search for buried nuts.

● Sometimes these wary birds visit gardens in the early morning, when they are less likely to be disturbed.

Ground beetles

Fast-moving ground beetles are among the few insects that are regularly seen out and about in winter. Many are ferocious carnivores that prey on slugs, snails and other garden pests.

With their glossy bodies, long legs and impressive turn of speed, ground beetles are among the more conspicuous insects to be found in parks and gardens, especially in winter when many other insects are in hiding. Although some ground beetles become dormant in especially cold weather, most of the 350 or so species found in the British Isles are active throughout the year.

All ground beetles belong to the family Carabidae, and are closely related to tiger beetles. They have a characteristic shape when viewed from above, because the thorax is protected by a plate-like thoracic shield, and is usually well separated from the wing cases by a distinct 'waist'.

Iridescent sheen
Most ground beetles are nocturnal and have rather sombre colours, although many are black with a metallic sheen. Ground beetles that are active during the daytime, such as *Callistus lunatus*, tend to be more colourful. A few have brilliant iridescent colours – none more impressive than those of the tree-dwelling *Calosoma sycophanta*, which is a rare visitor to the British Isles, mainly in summer.

However, not all the brightly coloured or metallic species are active by day. The beautiful green or blue *Harpalus aeneus* is rarely seen until nightfall.

At a length of 25–30mm (1–1¼in), the violet ground beetle, *Carabus violaceus*, is the largest of the British species. It can move very fast in pursuit of prey and uses its powerful jaws to crush small insects.

True to their name, most of these beetles spend their lives entirely on the ground, although some actually live in trees. Few low-level habitats are without their share of these active hunters. Several species are flightless. Unlike most beetles, they have no functional wings and some have hardened wing cases that are fused together. This provides them with extra protection while they are scuffling about in the soil or leaf litter in search of prey.

The shiny, black pterostichid beetles and the large carabid beetles – which include the violet ground beetle – are abundant in parks and gardens, as well as in woodlands and hedge-banks. Gardens also support the tiny *Notiophilus biguttatus*, just 6mm (¼in) long, identifiable by its bulging eyes. This sun-loving beetle prefers fairly open areas and can often be found on paths and bare ground.

Elaphrus riparius is one of several very small ground beetles that hunt on the muddy margins of ponds and streams, and can be found in such places in many parks. *Nebria complanata* is a coastal species, which lives around the shores of south-western England.

Most ground beetles are essentially predatory insects, and much of their prey consists of springtails, spiders, mites, slugs and small insects. *Cychrus caraboides* specialises in snails, and its narrow head

Unusually among ground beetles, the beautiful *Calosoma sycophanta* can fly. This continental species occasionally reaches the British Isles, where it can be found up in trees hunting for caterpillars.

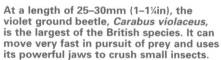

◄ The beautiful, brilliant metallic *Carabus auratus* is common in many parks and gardens. It is a recent colonist from Europe, having arrived some 25 years ago and spread through the south of England.

◄ The pale *Nebria complanata* lives mainly on sand dunes on the coasts of south-western Britain. It can be found during the daytime by turning over stones and debris near the shore.

beetles are truly omnivorous, and several are known as 'strawberry beetles' because of their preference for that fruit.

The antennae play an important role in seeking food, so they must be cleaned regularly. Many ground beetles achieve this by drawing their antennae through a conspicuous notch on each foreleg to remove debris.

▲ *Elaphrus riparius* is easiest to see on warm, sunny days. This brown beetle may be found in the margins of ponds and streams, where it hunts actively on the damp open ground.

Predatory larvae

and thorax are ideal for reaching into the shells of its prey. Several eat carrion, while others have a taste for vegetable food, including fruit and especially seeds. Those few ground beetles that live in trees pluck caterpillars from leaves or loose bark.

Members of the mainly vegetarian genus *Harpalus* can often be found exploring herbaceous plants. Pterostichid

The shuttle-shaped larvae of most ground beetles are also active hunters. Most pass through three larval stages or 'instars' before pupating – although some have only two larval instars, while others have as many as five. They are fairly long-lived insects, with many species surviving for at least two or even three years as adult beetles.

▲ Like the adults, most ground beetle larvae are active predators, catching and eating other soft-bodied invertebrates, such as slugs and worms. They take from several weeks to almost a year to reach maturity, and then pupate in the soil.

BOMBARDIER'S SECRET WEAPON

The bombardier has developed a unique form of self-defence, repelling attackers with a toxic spray. It is found mainly in coastal areas in southern Britain, but occurs on chalk grassland elsewhere.

Many ground beetles are able to defend themselves by discharging volatile, irritant fluids from glands at the tips of their tails. They may also regurgitate their gut contents, or produce disconcerting squeaks or buzzes.

The most dramatic defensive weapon belongs to the bombardier beetle, *Brachinus crepitans*. When alarmed, it fires a jet of steaming, corrosive fluid from its rear end, which disables small predators immediately, or drives them away. The volatile material cannot be stored, so the beetle produces it when required and discharges it straight away.

A mixture of relatively harmless ingredients is stored until needed, and then passed into a 'combustion chamber'. Enzymes secreted by the walls of the chamber bring about an instantaneous reaction, producing oxygen and water as well as the corrosive fluid. The reaction also produces sufficient heat to evaporate some of the fluid, triggering an explosion that forces it out through the beetle's anus with an audible pop and a puff of smoke. The beetle can produce up to 20 of these bursts in quick succession.

Recognising mosses and liverworts

These diminutive, flowerless plants form a miniature world of great beauty. Providing food and shelter for beetles and spiders, mosses and liverworts are also used by songbirds and small mammals to help build nests.

▲ **The bank hair moss *Polytrichum commune* is widespread, but most commonly found in the north and west.**

◄ **The delicate female reproductive structures of the common ribbon liverwort *Marchantia polymorpha* resemble miniature palm trees.**

The mild, wet climate of Britain and Ireland suits mosses and their relatives the liverworts extremely well. About 750 species of mosses and almost 300 of liverworts are scattered throughout these islands, making up about 60 per cent of the total for the whole of Europe. Some are very rare and found in just a few places, but many are wide-ranging. They thrive in wetter areas, such as the West Country, the Lake District, Wales and Ireland. North Wales, for example, serves as home to around three-quarters of all the mosses and liverworts in the whole of Britain.

Although mosses and liverworts continue to grow and stay green throughout the year, winter is a good time to look for them, because the foliage of most other plants that might overshadow them has died down. Among the simplest of all land plants, the great majority are small, only a few centimetres tall or long. Some, though, are much larger, such as the largest land species, the common bank hair moss *Polytrichum commune*, which grows in the wet, acid, peaty soils of bogs, fens,

heaths and birch woodland, and reaches up to 40cm (16in) tall.

Delicate anchors

Unlike the great majority of other land plants, mosses and liverworts do not produce flowers or seeds, reproducing instead by means of spores, in a similar way to ferns. They also lack a highly developed system for transporting water and food, such as those found in more complex land plants, and they have no roots. Instead, mosses and liverworts have thread-like rhizoids to anchor them to their growing surface. These are delicate parts, just one cell thick.

Mosses have distinct leaves attached to stems while most liverworts appear flat. Instead of differentiating between stem and leaf, botanists use the term 'thallus' to cover the entire liverwort structure. Consequently, liverworts are known as thallose plants.

The name liverwort is an old one. Herbalists of the Middle Ages thought the larger species resembled the lobed shape of the human liver and, in keeping with the medical lore of the time, used it to treat disorders of that organ.

WILDLIFE WATCH

Where can I find mosses and liverworts?

● Parks, gardens, city streets, remote moors, heaths and ancient woodland all support mosses and liverworts. They are able to colonise soil, rocks, tree trunks and branches, the tops of walls and even cracks between paving stones. These plants mostly thrive in moist, often shady, conditions, but very few can live submerged in water and there are none in the sea.

● A small proportion of mosses and liverworts can survive some drying out, and live in drier habitats than the majority, such as the select band of species that may be found on sand dunes.

EASY GUIDE TO SPOTTING MOSSES AND LIVERWORTS

WHAT ARE MOSSES AND LIVERWORTS?

● Mosses are placed in the class Musci while liverworts are in the class Hepaticae. Both belong to the major order Bryophyta, and together they are usually referred to by botanists as 'bryophytes'.

● Liverworts and mosses undergo what is known as an alternation of generations, existing in two different reproductive forms. One form is sexual – known as the gametophyte generation – which alternates throughout the life of the plant with an asexual form – the sporophyte generation. In liverworts, the gametophyte takes the form of a lobed thallus or leaf, while in mosses it is the leafy plant, in contrast to the spore-bearing capsules.

● During spring or autumn, depending on the species, mosses and liverworts bear sexual organs. Male antheridia produce mobile male sex cells, called antherozoids, which swim

in a film of water to the female egg-bearing archegonia to fertilise the eggs. In some species, the same plant will create both antherozoids and archegonia, while others have separate male and female plants.

● After the eggs have been fertilised, the resulting sporophytes grow up attached to the gametophyte. These sporophytes consist of a stalk (or seta) bearing a capsule in which more spores develop. The spores are eventually released and dispersed, usually blown by the wind. Under suitable conditions, these scattered spores germinate and grow into a new generation of gametophyte plants.

● Mosses and liverworts may also reproduce by shedding fragments of leaves or thalli, each of which can grow into a new plant. In some, specialised groups of cells called gemmae are produced for this purpose.

HOW CAN I IDENTIFY MOSSES AND LIVERWORTS?

● Useful clues that help to distinguish species are the shape, size and colour of thalli or leaves. Use a good-quality hand lens from a natural history equipment supplier to see whether minute hairs and other tiny features are present. Look at how the stems branch and note the distinctive appearance of male and female sex organs.

● Mosses mainly grow in one of two forms. Cushion mosses form compact pads of short upright stems that grow bunched tightly together, while feather mosses have much longer, trailing stems and a looser overall shape.

● The appearance of ripe spore capsules offers the best feature for identifying mosses. The

colour and shape of the capsule itself are important identifiers among the different species, and also the angle created at the point where the stalks rise up, and whether they stand erect or curve upwards.

● Spore capsules of liverworts have a very short season and release their contents simply by splitting along four axes. Those of mosses remain on the plant for a much longer length of time and, when they do ripen, have more complex mechanisms for releasing their spores. These involve the opening of protective hoods and lids, and often also teeth that surround the capsule mouth. Changes in humidity trigger these mechanisms to liberate the spores, which are sometimes shot out forcefully.

Distribution map key

 Present all year round

Not present

WAVY-LEAVED THREAD MOSS *Atrichum undulatum*

This large, erect moss, also known as Catherine's moss, has tall, unbranched stems bearing long, tapering, stiff, sharp-tipped leaves of variable colour, from pale to very dark green. They have minute teeth along their margins, visible with a hand lens.

The leaves have distinctly wavy edges that give this moss one of its common names.

● SIZE
Up to 10cm (4in) tall

● SPORE CAPSULES
Curved capsules form at an angle on long red stalks in late autumn and winter. They have lids with long beaks

● HABITAT
Common in damp places in woods, parks, gardens, fields, heaths and on stream banks

SILKY PENDULOUS THREAD MOSS *Pohlia nutans*

Two main types of leaves are produced by the silky pendulous thread moss – small ones, pointed at the tip, grow lower down and, higher up, longer ones with minute teeth at the edges taper to a lance-shaped point. This moss grows in loose, mid-green tufts.

Stiff, erect shoots with small brittle leaves that break off to form new plants enable the moss to spread.

● SIZE
Up to 4cm (1½in) tall

● SPORE CAPSULES
Green, bean-shaped capsules form in January and February, droop from long red stalks and turn brown when ripe

● HABITAT
Common in woods, parks and gardens along paths and other sites, mainly on acid soils

SWAN'S-NECK THREAD MOSS *Mnium hornum*

This widespread woodland moss forms large cushions on stumps and fallen timber. The leaves end in a sharp point. Male and female organs are borne on separate plants. In spring, flower-like rosettes of leaves enclose the male sexual organs.

The large, dark green leaves of this moss are edged with minute paired teeth.

● SIZE
Up to 10cm (4in) tall

● SPORE CAPSULES
Pale green in spring, then green above yellowish below, hanging on a long curving reddish stalk

● HABITAT
Very common in woods, parks and gardens on acid soils

SILVERY THREAD MOSS *Bryum argenteum*

This small moss grows in compact dark green mats or tufts that have a distinctive silvery sheen. Its tiny oval leaves, which are markedly concave and sharply pointed, clasp the stems tightly.

The leaves are mostly green but, except in wetter habitats, have shiny colourless tips that give the plant a catkin-like appearance.

● SIZE
Less than 1.5cm (⅝in) tall

● SPORE CAPSULES
Not often produced; small, drooping on short stalk; bright red when young, crimson-brown when mature

● HABITAT
Widespread and very common in many habitats, including city parks and gardens

CURLY THATCH MOSS *Dicranoweisia cirrata*

Curly thatch moss grows in small, neat, closely packed cushions. Its narrow, lance-shaped leaves taper gradually to a point. The leaves spread out when moist but curl in tightly and acquire a silvery sheen when dry.

The long leaves of this common lowland moss have smooth margins, unlike the minute teeth found in other species.

● SIZE
1–2cm (½–¾in) tall

● SPORE CAPSULES
Large curved spore capsules form in late autumn and last all winter; green when young, ripening to pale brown, they are held erect on long pale yellowish green stalks

● HABITAT
Common on tree trunks and branches, logs and fenceposts

SILKY FORK MOSS *Dicranella heteromalla*

Silky fork moss is found at the base of trees, on banks and in other shady places. The very narrow, curving leaves are borne on branching stems and taper to fine points. Female plants have more strongly curved leaves than those on male plants.

Silky fork moss grows in large, dark green, or occasionally yellowish, patches.

● SIZE
Up to 4cm (1½in) tall

● SPORE CAPSULES
Slightly curved, held almost horizontally on yellow stalks; striking orange in winter; lids fall to reveal reddish teeth

● HABITAT
Very common in parks, gardens, woods, shady banks and elsewhere except on chalky soils

DROOPING-LEAVED FEATHER MOSS *Rhytidiadelphus squarrosus*

Often forming extensive carpets, drooping-leaved feather moss has pale green or yellowish leaves that are only slightly twisted when dry. They point backwards towards reddish stems, which can be seen through the translucent leaves when the plants are held up to the light.

The leaves of drooping-leaved feather moss are broad-based and taper to finely pointed tips.

● SIZE
Up to 15cm (6in) long

● SPORE CAPSULES
Very rarely produced; roughly egg-shaped, horizontal or slightly drooping

● HABITAT
Chalk grassland, roadside verges, fields, open woodland, often in parks and on lawns, especially in moister areas and where fertiliser not used

COMMON CORD MOSS *Funaria hygrometrica*

Low tufts or carpets of common cord moss are an everyday sight in parks and forests. The crowded pale green or yellowish leaves are broadly oval and closely overlapping on the upper portions of the short stems.

Common cord moss is frequently found on soil that has been burnt, either on the surface or just beneath it.

● SIZE
Up to 3cm (1¼in) tall

● SPORE CAPSULES
Long swollen capsules form on a curving yellow stalk; pale orange when ripe in autumn and winter

● HABITAT
Parks, gardens, banks, walls and open woodland

WALL SCREW MOSS *Tortula muralis*

Small, neat cushions are formed on stones and rocks by wall screw moss. The leaves are tongue-shaped, deep green or bright yellowish, with well-developed midribs, and they end in long, hair-like, silvery points.

The leaves of this very common moss are widely spaced when moist and twisted when dry.

● **SIZE**
Up to 1cm (½in) tall

● **SPORE CAPSULES**
Upright, on short stalk; yellow when young, turning purplish red with age; long spirally twisted hair-like teeth visible when lid falls off

● **HABITAT**
Walls and stones, including those in towns and cities

RIBBON LIVERWORT *Marchantia polymorpha*

This large liverwort has a distinctive midrib, and the surface of the thallus is covered with a hexagonal pattern. It reproduces asexually from gemmae, tiny ball-like structures produced in tooth-edged cups.

The female sexual organs, or carpophores, consist of 8–10 narrow rays radiating from a central disc, borne on a long stalk.

● **SIZE**
Up to 10cm (4in) long, 1.3cm (½in) wide

● **SPORE CAPSULES**
Groups of capsules appear in summer beneath the arms of the star-like female organs

● **HABITAT**
Damper areas in parks and gardens; streamsides, especially with steep, clay banks; bogs

WIDE-NERVED LIVERWORT *Pellia epiphylla*

Male and female sex organs are borne on the same plant in this very common species. Bumps, often reddish in colour, conceal the male organs in tiny pits on the upper surface, while the female ones appear under minute green flaps above the midrib.

The forked and strongly lobed rich green branches show broad but rather indistinct midribs.

● **SIZE**
10cm (4in) long and up to 1cm (½in) wide

● **SPORE CAPSULES**
Many greenish black capsules on long thin stalks appear in early spring; soon split to reveal spores entangled in brown hairs

● **HABITAT**
Damp, lime-free spots in parks, gardens, woods and other habitats, such as stream banks

GREAT SCENTED LIVERWORT *Conocephalum conicum*

A very large, dark green thallose plant, the great scented liverwort forms large, flat patches and has a characteristic fragrant smell when bruised. Conical female sex organs are borne on long stalks, male ones in small purplish cushions near the tips of branches.

The upper surface of the great scented liverwort bears slightly raised breathing pores.

● **SIZE**
Up to 15cm (6in) long, 2cm (¾in) wide

● **SPORE CAPSULES**
Conical capsules appear in spring; green at first, they soon turn purple

● **HABITAT**
Common on damp walls and rocks in shady places, including in and by streams

SPLEENWORT LEAFY LIVERWORT *Plagiochila asplenioides*

One of the commonest of the leafy liverworts, this is also one of the biggest. The leaves are large and oval, and usually have finely toothed edges. An even larger variety of this species has overlapping leaves.

Tufts of rather stiff, more or less upright shoots grow from almost leafless, prostrate stems.

● **SIZE**
10cm (4in) long and 1cm (½in) wide

● **SPORE CAPSULES**
Brown oval capsules develop within sheaths and emerge on pale brownish stalks in spring

● **HABITAT**
Damp places in woods, parks, gardens and elsewhere on a wide range of soil types

The mistletoe

Many myths and legends are associated with mistletoe, not least that it lives off thin air. In fact, this plant is parasitic, taking nutrients from host shrubs and trees such as apple, lime and poplar.

Winter is the best time of year to see mistletoe growing in its natural setting. The plant forms bushy tufts, about 50–200cm (20–80in) across, in the tops of deciduous trees. These balls of evergreen foliage are clearly visible among the leafless branches.

It is at this time of year that mistletoe produces soft, white berries, which are eagerly consumed by birds, such as mistle thrushes. The birds devour the flesh of the berries but the seeds tend to stick to their beaks. To remove the seeds, they scrape their beaks on the branches of trees. In this way the seeds are carried to other trees and implanted into ideal germination sites.

Invading suckers

Germination occurs in early spring. Each mistletoe seed sprouts, putting out suckers that invade the host for nourishment, plumbing themselves into the water-conducting tissue, or xylem, of the tree. Mistletoe absorbs water and mineral nutrients from its host but it manufactures its own sugars and starch within its green

► **Mistletoe forms dense balls of foliage high in deciduous trees. Without roots or an obvious source of food, the plant acquired an aura of mysticism.**

◄ **The white berries of mistletoe are plump and rounded, with a layer of sticky flesh around the single seed. They ripen from November to December.**

leaves. It is therefore known by botanists as a hemi-parasite (partial parasite) rather than a wholly parasitic plant.

Mistletoe is a woodland plant found across most of Europe, except the far north and east, and south-western Asia. In Britain, it is at its natural northern limit in mid-Wales and the Midlands, extending into parts of Yorkshire, but its heartland is Gloucestershire and the Welsh borders – Herefordshire and Worcestershire in particular. It is absent from Ireland, apart from a few colonies around Dublin that have probably been introduced.

Botanists have recorded mistletoe on more than 200 species of host trees or shrubs in Britain. Apple is by far the commonest host, followed by poplars and lime. Apple belongs to the rose family and mistletoe also grows on related trees, such as hawthorn, cotoneaster, ornamental cherries, japonica and rowan, but much less often. It has even occurred on large wild rose bushes.

Only rarely does mistletoe grow on conifers in Britain, but in the Alps and the

MISTLETOE FACT FILE

A woody evergreen shrub, mistletoe is partially parasitic on a wide range of soft-wooded deciduous trees, but rarely evergreens.

● **NAMES**
Common name: mistletoe
Scientific name: *Viscum album*

● **HABITAT**
Deciduous trees and shrubs, rarely conifers

● **DISTRIBUTION**
Throughout most of England and Wales; absent from Scotland and Ireland

● **SIZE**
Clusters of varying size, from 0.5–2m (1½–6½ft) across; stems up to 1m (3ft) long

● **KEY FEATURES**
Forms rounded clusters of numerous, forked, quite woody green stems in branches of host trees; grows slowly for the first 3 or 4 years then at a faster rate

● **LEAVES**
Leathery, blunt, yellow-green and usually paired, up to 8cm (3in) long

● **FRUIT**
Round berries start off opaque green, turning white then translucent when ripe (in November–December)

● **FLOWERS**
Small, yellowish green flowers with 4 petals, held in clusters of 3–5; appear February–April; the plant does not flower until at least 7 years old

Elliptical leaves grow in pairs.

Tiny flowers have four petals.

Clusters of sticky, white berries form in forks.

The inconspicuous yellow flowers secrete nectar and are pollinated by flies. Male and female flowers are borne on separate plants.

Where can I see mistletoe?

● Mistletoe can easily be spotted against the winter skyline once the trees have shed their leaves.

● Old orchards and parks sometimes have large quantities of mistletoe, especially in southern England and the English side of the Welsh border.

● Each winter, in the four weeks before Christmas, mistletoe and holly are sold in bulk at a special market in Tenbury Wells, Worcestershire.

DID YOU KNOW?

Another species of mistletoe, *Viscum cruciatum*, found in southern Spain and North Africa, has red berries. It grows on wild olive trees.

Mediterranean region a separate subspecies of mistletoe sometimes grows in ancient fir trees.

Due to mistletoe's close association with apple trees, it has been a useful by-product of mature orchards for the past 150 years. Today great quantities of Christmas mistletoe are imported into Britain from cider orchards in Normandy to supplement supplies of native mistletoe from the old Herefordshire and Worcestershire orchards.

Pagan past

Mistletoe also grows on oak, and the ancient druids attributed sacred significance to this, cutting the plant down with a golden sickle and using it in various rites. They believed the plant protected against evil. It was because of its association with the druids

and even older pagan rituals that the early Christian church banned the use of mistletoe.

Records of mistletoe being revered as a magical, healing plant are found all over Europe. The green leafy growth on apparently dead boughs of trees made the species a potent symbol of life in the depths of winter. It was often used in fertility rituals and the Christmas tradition of kissing under the mistletoe is a vestige of this ancient belief.

Recent German research has shown that chemical constituents of mistletoe stimulate the immune system and inhibit the growth of tumours. Clinical trials are still under way, but it seems that mistletoe's reported healing powers are not unfounded.

◄ The mistle thrush derives its name from its preference for mistletoe berries. The berries, like those of holly and yew, are an important winter food.

▲ Dense balls of mistletoe are often found high up in the top-most branches of host trees. Their seeds have been placed there by berry-eating birds.

The yew tree

From the ancient trees that have stood in churchyards for centuries to the fanciful creations of topiary gardens, yew has many uses. Even the poisons in its foliage may, if used in the right way, help to save lives.

Dark, deadly and capable of living to an almost inconceivable age, the yew is a tree of mystery, danger and even magic. In the dead of winter, when snow blankets the ground and most native trees are bare and skeletal, the yew remains almost unnaturally glossy and vital. In 1658, the author Sir Thomas Browne attributed its presence in many churchyards to this 'perpetual verdure', seeing it as an emblem of resurrection. Yet sophisticated dating techniques suggest that some churchyard yews are several thousand years old, far older than the churches built alongside them. It seems that they may have been planted in prehistory, for ritual reasons that can only be surmised. They are survivors from a lost world.

Heavy shade

The yew is one of just three needle-leaved evergreen trees that are native to Britain. The other two are juniper and Scots pine. Although it can be found on different soils, and in various types of mixed woodland, its stronghold is on free-draining chalk soils, such as the southern downlands. Here, particularly on the slopes where woodland meets grassland, the soils are very poor, yet the yew thrives and even dominates other species. The trees cast such heavy shade that other plants struggle to compete. For example, a search among the branches of a yew may reveal the dead stumps of juniper – another pioneer of chalk downland that initially encourages yew to colonise, and then succumbs to it.

Once established, the yew spreads to nearby exposed locations where its seedlings seem to cope better with dry conditions than those of other trees. They grow rapidly during their early life, increasing their height by 20–30cm (8–12in) a year, but slow down with advancing age.

The central trunk of a mature tree is usually deeply ribbed and fluted, owing to many shoots sprouting from the base and fusing together. If a yew reaches an age where its spreading, low-growing boughs touch the ground, new roots develop at the point of contact. New shoots then grow upward, and as a result many ancient yew trees have several trunks. They resemble rings of separate trees, each with many low-growing branches, but are actually offshoots of a single tree, growing with renewed vigour. This is one reason why yews can achieve such great age.

Dense and resilient, and able to sprout from old wood after heavy pruning, yew makes an ideal plant for topiary and ornamental hedging. Such topiary gardens can be a spectacular sight when dusted with snow in winter.

YEW TREE FACT FILE

A large and often stately tree, the yew has dense, dark foliage of flattened, needle-like leaves. If left untouched, it forms a tall, conical tree, but it is often trimmed for hedging or topiary. Mature trees have extremely broad trunks and long, spreading lower branches.

● **NAMES**
Common names: yew, common yew
Scientific name: *Taxus baccata*

● **HABITAT**
Mainly on well-drained chalk soils; often planted in parks and gardens

● **DISTRIBUTION**
Throughout Britain and Ireland

● **HEIGHT**
Up to 25m (80ft)

● **LIFESPAN**
May live to at least 5000 years, possibly longer

● **BARK**
Reddish, greyish and purplish, often gnarled and peeling in mature trees

● **LEAVES**
Tough and resistant needles that are flattened and dark green above, dull yellowish green beneath; about 3cm (1¼in) long and 3mm (⅛in) wide with pointed tip; toxic

● **TWIGS**
Green when young, brown when older, with bark that flakes with age

● **FLOWERS**
Male and female flowers are borne on separate trees; male flowers comprise solitary clusters of yellow anthers; female flowers are green

● **FRUITS**
Fertilised female flowers give rise to hard fruits that are covered by a fleshy, red, berry-like structure, called an aril, with a round depression at the tip

● **USES**
Planted for hedging or topiary; timber once popular for furniture and decorative carving

Yew fruits are not true berries, because they do not completely enclose the seeds. The seeds are extremely poisonous, as are most other parts of the tree, including the bark and leaves.

Branches are broadly spreading but invariably conform to the overall conical shape of the tree.

Leaves arise spirally along the stem but are flattened to lie in a row on either side of the twig.

The yew tree has a broad base but often appears of even width up to the level of the first branches.

FLOWERS & FRUITS

Yew trees bear either male or female flowers. The male flowers are small, yellow and ball-shaped and – like the female flowers – grow in clusters at the base of the needles. The male trees produce vast amounts of pollen when they are in flower from February to April. Clouds of pollen are carried on the wind, and some eventually lands on female trees where they pollinate the female flowers.

These are small bud-like structures that, once pollinated, swell to form the fleshy fruits. Green at first, they turn red by mid-September. The soft red flesh of each fruit surrounds the single hard seed, which is greenish black and exposed at the open end.

Male flowers are simple structures comprising only anthers, which release the pollen.

Seed dispersal

The yew is 'dioecious', which means that the male and female flowers always appear on separate trees. Only the flowers of female trees develop into yew berries – or arils as they are correctly known.

These soft, sticky, bright red fruits are extremely attractive to birds, particularly members of the thrush family. Starlings, greenfinches, great tits and coal tits also eat large numbers of them.

The red flesh is nutritious, but the seeds are poisonous. Luckily for the birds, seeds swallowed whole are indigestible, so they – and the birds – survive their journey through the birds' digestive systems. The birds then void the seeds in their droppings, dispersing them well away from the parent tree. Dropped to the ground with a dose of avian fertiliser, each seed soon sprouts into a new young tree.

Gall midge

The yew is not renowned for supporting many insects or other invertebrates. However, artichoke galls can often be found on the tips of branches. These are caused by a minute fly called the yew midge. The life cycle of this tiny gall midge takes two years to complete, with the galls visible during the second year. Initially, each female lays up to 160 eggs singly on the underside of new leaf shoots.

The eggs are bright orange and hatch within one or two weeks, usually in June. The young larvae then crawl to the terminal buds and burrow inside. The galls begin to develop, and grow up to 3cm (1¼in) long by the following July. The larvae overwinter in the galls, and emerge as adult midges in May, ready to mate and produce a new generation of eggs and larvae.

The yew provides food for only a few insects. They include the caterpillars of the black arches moth, shown here as they hatch from their eggs.

Life-saving toxins

Although yew foliage is poisonous, both domestic and wild animals occasionally browse on it. If they do so regularly, they may build up a degree of resistance to the toxins, although not to the point where they can eat any great quantity. The foliage is toxic to humans too, so it is best not to crush or even handle the leaves of ornamental yews or yew hedges. Furthermore, clippings left lying on the ground increase in toxicity as they wither.

However, the toxins have their positive side. They can be processed into a drug that is used against ovarian cancer. Immense quantities of yew are needed to produce small amounts of the drug, though, making it extremely expensive.

ANCIENT YEWS

◄ The Fortingall yew in Scotland may be more than 5000 years old, and is one of the oldest surviving yews in Britain.

The true age of ancient yews has caused much speculation. While it is clear that many yews have survived for centuries, some naturalists believe that the oldest trees are several thousand years old. If so, then they could be the oldest living things in Europe.

Once a yew is some 400 to 500 years old, the middle of the tree starts to hollow out. This can make it appear as if the tree is about to die, or is becoming dangerous. This is rarely the case, however, because many trees can last for centuries in this condition, sprouting new shoots from the living parts of the trunk. It does, however, pose a problem when trying to determine the true age of the tree.

Most trees can be aged by counting the annual growth rings, but this cannot be done on an ancient yew. Fortunately, the yew's antiquity also fascinated early naturalists, who took careful measurements of particular trees. These can be compared with modern data to provide estimates of the trees' ages.

For example, the yew tree at Fortingall, Perthshire, was measured in 1769, and its circumference was very similar to its girth today. This very slow growth rate can be used to calculate the tree's age. Comparing the available tree-ring data with that of other yews that have blown down in storms suggests that the tree at Fortingall may be 5000 years old, and quite possibly older. Although the original trunk of this ancient yew has long since been reduced to a hollow shell, it has now been replaced by an outer ring of regrown stems, demonstrating the tree's remarkable powers of survival.

The yew trees of Kingley Vale in Sussex are at least five centuries old, but despite their wizened and gnarled state they could easily survive for another thousand years or more.

The yew midge makes a gall that looks like a kind of green cone sprouting from a tender yew shoot.

◄ The spreading branches and thick foliage of yew can provide sheltered, relatively secure nesting sites for birds such as this song thrush.

▶ Woodland birds, such as the great tit, roost and nest in yew trees, and search the foliage for insects. They also eat the fruits and spread the seeds.

▲ Yew trees provide shelter and food for greenfinches, which often feed in mixed flocks with other finches in winter.

Yew sculptures

Yew is highly valued as a hedging and topiary plant in parks and gardens, because of its density, stability and ability to recover well from hard clipping. Its relatively slow rate of growth once established is an asset, because the clipped yew holds its shape for a long time. These yew sculptures also have the merit of being equally striking in mid-winter, when other plants look dull or have died down altogether. The yew's tolerance to pollution makes it an ideal decorative tree or shrub for inner city parks.

The wood of the yew is the most densely grained of all timbers, and it is extremely durable. It used to be said that a fencepost made of yew could outlast one made of iron, and the world's oldest wooden artefact is a yew spear found at Clacton in Essex, estimated to be 150,000 years old. The wood is so hard that the Vikings used it for nails in the building of their ships. It has also been used for the teeth of cogwheels in mills.

The slippery jack fungus, recognisable by its orange-brown cap, can often be found beneath yew trees.

The most famous use for yew, however, was the longbow. The tree's scientific name *Taxus* is derived from the word *taxon*, meaning bow. Each longbow was made of a baulk of timber containing both the sap wood and the heartwood of the yew trunk, giving the weapon its lethal combination of strength and springiness. During the excavation of the sunken Tudor warship *Mary Rose*, 138 yew longbows – and 3500 arrows – were found in the wreck. Despite being submerged for more than 450 years, many of the bows were in apparently perfect and almost usable condition – a testament to the astonishing durability of the yew.

YEW CONSERVATION

● Old yew trees should be properly protected. The Yew Tree Campaign, started by the Conservation Foundation in 1987, suggests contacting the local authority to make sure that a Tree Preservation Order is in place to protect it. The Conservation Foundation can provide expert advice: contact Libby Symon on libbysymon@ conservationfoundation.co.uk

● Hollow yew trees tend to collect dead leaves, or may even be used to dump organic waste. As all this debris rots down, the inside of the tree will start to decay with it. The tree should be kept as clean as possible inside.

● The roots of a yew should be protected from damage as much as possible when excavation work is taking place.

● Resist the temptation for unnecessary tree surgery. Remember that these trees show a remarkable ability to survive without any human intervention. If you are concerned about the safety of an old tree, contact your local authority.

● Nearby trees, particularly holly and elder, can compete with yews. If the yew is more valuable, they should be cut back or even removed.

WILDLIFE WATCH

Where can I see yew trees?

There are many places across Britain where yew trees can be seen. Here are the some of the best sites to visit:

● Castle Drogo in Devon is a National Trust property with immense yew hedges, conceived as part of the architecture of the building.

● Hever Castle in Kent has spectacular yew topiary, including giant chessmen and a superb yew maze.

● At Packwood House in Warwickshire, the garden is overshadowed by towering yew topiary dating from the mid-18th century.

● Box Hill in Surrey, above the River Mole, has many yew trees. The site is owned by the National Trust.

● The yew at Fortingall in Glen Lyon, Perthshire, may be more than 5000 years old.

● Muckross Wood and Ross Island near Killarney in the Republic of Ireland have yews growing in mixed woodland. These limestone-rich sites are within a National Park.

● The yew wood at Kingley Vale near Chichester in Sussex is a National Nature Reserve with many old and splendidly gnarled trees.

● White Waltham churchyard near Maidenhead in Berkshire contains a tree considered to be 1600 years old.

● At Fountains Abbey, North Yorkshire, two trees remain of the seven that were reputedly used for shelter by the monks building the abbey.

● Although it is now dead, the famous Selborne yew described by the naturalist Gilbert White is still standing in the churchyard at Selborne, Hampshire.

Index

Acknowledgments

Photographs: Cover: Blue tit Woodfall Wild Images/Mike Lane, garden Andrew Lawson (Barnsley House, Glos). Back cover: wood mouse Woodfall Wild Images/Andrew Newman.
1 FLPA/H Clark; 2–3 Ardea/Joan Beames; 4 (t) OSF/Harold Taylor, (b) OSF/A Ramage; 5 Ardea /John Daniel; 6(bl) NP/EA Janes, (bc) NP, (br) NP/EA Janes; 7(bl) NP/B Burbidge, (bc) NP, (br) NP/EA Janes; 8(bl) NP/P Sterry, (bc) NP/P Sterry, (br) NP/EA Janes; 9(bl) NP/M Gore, (bc) NP, (br) NP/R Tidman; 10–11 Ardea/Duncan Usher; 12(tr) NP/PJ Newman, (cr) NP/G du Feu, (bl) NP/P Sterry; 13 NP; 14(cr) Ardea/J Mason, (bl) Garden World Images; 15(tl) Ardea/Ian Beames, (tr) Ardea/J Mason, (bl) NV/Heather Angel; 16(tl, cl) FLPA, (tr,b) Ardea; 17(tl) FLPA/T Wittaker, (tr,cr,b) FLPA; 18(c) NP/P Sterry, (b) NI/B Gibbons; 19(tl) Wildlife Matters/D Mezzereon, (cr) Wildlife Matters/D Laureola, (bl) Midsummer Books; 20(t) Ardea/John Daniels, (bl) Mike Read; 21(tl) FLPA, (tr,bl) Mike Read; 22(tl) Ardea/John Daniels, (b) Ardea/Richard Vaughan; 23(tl) BC/Kim Taylor, (tr) NHPA/Ernie Janes, (b) Ardea/Ian Beames; 24(tr) OSF/H Taylor, (b) Prema; 25(tl, tr, cr) Prema, (bc) OSF/D Boag; 26(l) NV/Heather Angel, (r) NP/A Cleave; 27(tr) NV/Heather Angel, (c) FLPA/T Hamblin, (cr) FLPA/HD Brandl, (br) FLPA/M Withers; 28(tl) NP/R Tidman, (tr) FLPA/R Tidman, (b) NV/Heather Angel; 29(tc) FLPA/J Thomas, (tr) NV/Heather Angel, (cr) FLPA/H Clark, (bl) NP/F Blackburn; 30(tc) FLPA, (tr) NP, (cl) NV/Heather Angel, (c) NP; 31(t) Laurie Campbell, (b) FLPA/E&D Hosking; 32(l) Corbis/Jason Hawkes; 33(tr) Rex Features/Ilpo Musho, (cl) NV/C.Andrew Henley, (br) Topfoto/Pressnet; 34(tru) Alamy/Edward Parker, (tr) Apex News/Simon Burt, (c) Apex News/Chris Saville, (bl) Alamy/Lavendelfoto/Interfoto; 35(tr) Alamy/Marc Hills/Apex News, (cl) NPL/Pete Oxford, (c,bc) NVHeather Angel, (br) Alamy/Elmtree Images; 36(tr) Alamy/Edward Parker, (bl) Ardea/Bob Gibbons, (bc) FLPA/Martin B Withers, (br) Ardea/Ake Lindau; 37(b) Alamy/Edward Parker; 38–39 Ardea/John Daniels; 40(t) OSF/Harold Taylor; 41(tc,tr) FLPA/R Tidman, (b) BC/Paul van Gaalen; 42(tl) FLPA/RP Lawrence, (tr) Ardea/Ian Beames, (c) FLPA/Silvestris; 43(tr) FLPA/R Tidman; 44(t) FLPA/Robert Canis; 45(t) FLPA/Martin H Smith, (c) FLPA/Roger Wilmhurst; 46(b) FLPA/H Clark; 47(tl) FLPA/Silvestris, (tr) BC/Hans Reinhard, (br) OSF/R Packwood; 48(tl) FLPA/Hugo Wilcox/Foto Natura, (tr) OSF/R Packwood; 49(tr) NV/Jason Venus, (b) Pat Morris; 50 Mike Read; 51(t,br) Mike Read, (b) NP/P Sterry; 52(b) Mike Read; 53 Mike Read; 54(t) NP/Paul Sterry, (br) Mike Read; 55(tr) NP/EA Janes, (cl) Mike Read, (br) NHPA/Eric Soder; 56(l) FLPA/A Faulkner-Taylor; 57(tr) FLPA/B Borrell, (bc,br) Aquila/MC Wilkes; 58(tl) FLPA/AR Hosking, (tr) Aquila/S Bassett, (cl) FLPA/R Wilmshurst, (c) FLPA/HD Brandel, (cr) FLPA/B Borrell, (bl) FLPA/E&D Hosking, (bc) FLPA/R Brooks, (br) Aquila/MC Wilkes; 59(tr) FLPA/R Bird, (cl) FLPA/MC Wilkes, (br) Aquila/R Wilmhurst; 60(cl,br) FLPA/S Magennis; 61(tr) FLPA, (cl,cr) Aquila; 62(b) Aquila/M Lane; 63(tr) OSF/D Fox; 64(bl) NPL/B Britton; 65(tl) Aquila/M Wilkes, (tc) FLPA/J Tinning, (tr) FLPA/M Jones; 65(cl) David Chapman, (c) FLPA/J Watkins, (cr) NP/R Tidman, (br) OSF/M Hamblin, (cr) Aquila/J Jones, (br) David Chapman; 67(b) BC/Kim Taylor; 68(tr,bl) PW, (br) BC/G Dore; 69(tr) BC/J Brackenbury, (bl) NP/ N Brown; 70(tl) PW, (tr) NHPA/NA Callow, (cl) NSc/P Ward, (cr) NV/Heather Angel; 71(tr) NP/P Sterry, (bl) NP/B Chapman; 72(tr, cr) Michael Chinery, (br) NP; 73(tl) Aquila, (tc) NI, (tr) Aquila, (c) Michael Chinery, (bl) Michael Chinery, (blu) NP, (br) NP; 74(tl) OSF/D Houghton, (tr) NP/P Sterry, (cr) NV, (br) FLPA/GE Hyde; 75(r) NPL/Tony Evans; 76(tl) FLPA/David T Grewcock, (tr) NHPA/EA Janes, (cr) NHPA/Helmut Moik, (br) FLPA/Winfried Wisnieski; 77(tl) NHPA/Laurie Campbell, (tr) Ardea/Steve Hopkin, (cr) NHPA/Mike Lane (b) OSF; 78(tl) OSF/Bob Gibbons, (tr) GPL/John Glover; 79(t,tc) NV/Heather Angel, (cr) Aquila/A Cardwell; 80(bl) OSF/T Heathcote, (br) NV/Heather Angel; 81(tr) Aquila/D Robinson, (br) FLPA/MJ Thomas; 82(tr) NV/Heather Angel, (cr,bl) FLPA/E&D Hosking; 83 Ardea/Ian Beames; 84(l) NPL/B Lightfoot; 85(tl) OSF/GI Bernard, (blu) OSF/D Houghton, (br) NV/Heather Angel; 86(tc) MJ Woods, (cl) NPL/B Lundberg, (c) NPL/T Phelps, (br) OSF/P Henry; 87(cl) NV/Heather Angel, (c) OSF/N Benvie, (cr) OSF/P Henry; 88(b) FLPA/R Bender; 90(tl) NP/EA Janes, (bl) NP/P Sterry; 91(tl) FLPA/Silvestris, (bl) NV/G Kinns; 92(tl) BC/R Williams, (bl) BC/N Blake; 93(tl) BC/G McCarthy, (c) BC/H Reinhard; 94(r) Midsummer Books/Paul Bricknell; 95(tl) NHPA/M Leach, (b) NHPA/S Dalton; 96(l) BC/H Reinhard; 97(tl) BC, (br) BC/WS Paton; 98(tl) BC/G McCarthy, (tr,bl) BC, (br) Unknown; 99(t,b) FLPA/R Wilmhurst; 100(tl) FLPA/Roger Wilmhurst, (c) Aquila/MC Wilkes; 101(tl) NP/P Newman, (bl) OSF/M Hamblin; 102(tl) David Chapman, (br) FLPA/R Wilmhurst; 103(tl,bl) FLPA/R Wilmhurst; 104(c) Windrush/L Borg; 105(tr) FLPA/R Wilmhurst, (r) Aquila/AT Moffett; 106(tl) BC/K Taylor, (tr) FLPA/H Clark; 107(tl, tr, cl, c, cr) Aquila, (tc) NSc/MW Powles, (b) FLPA/R Wilmhurst; 108(tl) FLPA/AR Hamblin, (tr,b) Aquila/AT Moffett, (cl) Planet Earth/Frank Blackburn; 109(tl) FLPA/GT Andrewartha, (tr) Aquila/AT Moffett, (br) Aquila/MC Wilkes; 110(b) NHPA/Manfred Danneger; 111(tr) Ardea/JA Bailey, (bl,br) FLPA/E&D Hosking; 112(tl) Ardea/Richard Vaughan, (tc) Windrush/EA Janes, (tr,c) Windrush/F Blackburn, (cl) FLPA/AR Hamblin, (cr) Warren Photographic; 113(bl) Warren Photographic/Kim Taylor, (br) FLPA/John Watkins; 114(tr) OSF/A Ramage, (bl) FLPA/B Borrell; 115(tl) FLPA/F Brandl, (tr) PW, (cl) Michael Chinery, (cr) OSF/I Cushing; (bl) NHPA/M Tweedie; 116(tl) NV/Heather Angel, (bl) OSF; 117(cu) NV/Heather Angel, (c) NHPA/Laurie Campbell, (bc) OSF; 118(tc,cu,c,bcu) NV/Heather Angel, (bc) FLPA/DP Wilson; 119(tc,cu,c,bcu) OSF, (bc) NP/P Sterry; 120(t) BC/H Reinhard, (bl) FLPA/R Wilmhurst; 121(tc) Andrew Gagg, (bl) FLPA/R Tidman, (br) NV/Heather Angel; 122(b) GPL/John Glover; 123(bl,br) NV/Heather Angel; 124(tr) NPL/Hans Christophe Kappel, (blu) Ardea, (bl,br) NV/Heather Angel; 125(tl,tr,c) Ardea, (tc) FLPA.

Illustrations: 42-5 John Ridyard; 48(b) John Ridyard; 52 Dan Cole/Wildlife Art Agency; 59-60 John Ridyard; 64-66 John Ridyard; 87(t) John Ridyard; 89-90 Guy Troughton; 96-7 John Ridyard; 101-102 Tim Hayward; 106-7 John Ridyard; 113(t) John Ridyard; 123-4 Ian Garrard.

Key to Photo Library Abbreviations: BC = Bruce Coleman Ltd, FLPA = Frank Lane Photo Agency, GPL = Garden Picture Library; NHPA = Natural History Photo Agency, NI= Natural Image, NP = Nature Photographers, NPL = Nature Picture Library, NSc = Natural Science Photos, NV = Heather Angel/Natural Visions, OSF = Oxford Scientific Films, PW = Premaphotos Wildlife, WW = Woodfall Wild.

Key to position abbreviations: b = bottom, bl = bottom left, blu = bottom left upper, br = bottom right, bru = bottom right upper, c = centre, cl = centre left, clu = centre left upper, cr = centre right, cru = centre right upper, cu = centre upper, l = left, r = right, sp = spread, t = top, tl = top left, tlu = top left upper, tr = top right, tru = top right upper.

Wildlife Watch

Gardens & Parks in Winter

Published by the Reader's Digest Association Limited, 2005

The Reader's Digest Association Limited
11 Westferry Circus, Canary Wharf
London E14 4HE

Reprinted 2005

We are committed to both the quality of our products and the service we provide to our customers, so please feel free to contact us on 08705 113366, or via our website at: www.readersdigest.co.uk

If you have any comments about the content of our books you can contact us at: gbeditorial@readersdigest.co.uk

® Reader's Digest, The Digest and the Pegasus logo are registered trademarks of The Reader's Digest Association, Inc., of Pleasantville, New York, USA

Reader's Digest General Books:
Editorial Director Julian Browne
Art Director Nick Clark
Managing Editor Alastair Holmes
Series Editor Christine Noble
Project Editor Lisa Thomas
Project Art Editor Julie Bennett
Prepress Accounts Manager Penelope Grose

This book was designed, edited and produced by Eaglemoss Publications Ltd, based on material first published as the partwork *Wildlife of Britain*

For Eaglemoss:
Project Editor Marion Paull
Editors Celia Coyne, Helen Spence, John Woodward
Art Editor Phil Gibbs
Editorial Assistant Helen Hawksfield
Consultant Jonathan Elphick

Publishing Manager Nina Hathway

Copyright © Eaglemoss Publications Ltd/Midsummer Books Ltd 2005

Printed and bound in Europe by Arvato Iberia

CONCEPT CODE: UK 0133/G/S
BOOK CODE: 630-008-02
ISBN: 0 276 44056 0
ORACLE CODE: 356200007H.00.24